THE TEMPLE
IN CREATION

A PORTRAIT OF THE FAMILY
DINAH DYE

So often people will ask me why I never teach the deep spiritual meanings of the Scriptures, and my reply is always the same: "Why on earth would I do that when I can send the people seeking such things to Dinah Dye instead?" In *The Temple Revealed in Creation: A Portrait of the Family*, Dinah does what she does best — she redirects our modern minds toward the world of those to whom the Scriptures were actually written. It doesn't matter what Revelation means to us, what we think Messiah and the Prophets were saying, or our personal feelings about the Temple and its services — the vital question we should be asking is, "What did this mean to the people whose very lives were centered around the Temple in Jerusalem, its G-d, and a deep longing for Messiah?" It is my genuine hope that you will allow Dinah to awaken within you a love for the most complex, vital, and pervasive theme in all of Scripture — the Holy Temple and its service.

TYLER DAWN ROSENQUIST, AUTHOR

ANCIENT BRIDGE PUBLISHING

This new book by Dr. Dinah Dye marks a new milestone in books about the Temple. From the first page, the reader is in the midst of the story — not just learning the ancient principles and understandings long forgotten, but experiencing the sights, smells and sensations that bring the Temple to life. Dr. Dye's skill in showing the Temple, from the first Hebrew word of Scripture, opens up a world of new Temple revelation that also ties to concepts of the family and marriage. Few books have the potential this does to transform the reader into a different person with an elevated perception of the Kingdom of Heaven. Well done, Dinah!

JOSEPH GOOD, AUTHOR

HATIKVA MINISTRIES

JERUSALEM TEMPLE STUDY ONLINE

Brilliant! Dr. Dinah Dye's research on the Temple is second-to-none. I was immediately drawn into the story of the Temple. I found this book to be superior to the material currently available on this topic. Dinah has combined the elements of great story-telling with in-depth research, making this book a must-read!

DR. RIK B. WADGE, AUTHOR
EXECUTIVE DIRECTOR, BIBLEINTERACT

Dr. Dinah Dye has done an amazing job connecting ancient near eastern thought, rabbinical writings, and other important scholarly information to bring a broader perspective on the importance of the Temple and its functions. I really enjoyed the information and found myself getting lost in the story line. This work is filled with much needed information about the Temple.

RICO CORTES, SPEAKER/TEACHER
WISDOM IN TORAH

A compelling journey with a learned bible detective into the shadow and types of the Temple. Amazing revelation about the "creation covenant" and G-d's plan for families through the imagery of the ancient Temple rituals. Profoundly relevant today in light of the attack against families. You will never look at the Temple the same again!

JANE BAKEWELL
FREELANCE JOURNALIST & LOVER OF ISRAEL

For too long the Temple has been a mystery or simply ignored by many in the Church. In 2014, I was one of the participants from New Mexico who celebrated *Sukkot* in Israel and happened upon the re-enactment of the *Simcha Beit HaShoevah* — the Rejoicing in the House of the Water Drawing. Though I rejoiced in being part of this event (which last took place 2000 years ago), there was a certain regret at not fully understanding its significance. This birthed in me a hunger and determination to learn more. Dr. Dinah Dye has invested many years of research and study and the result is phenomenal. In this first volume, *The Temple Revealed in Creation*, she has laid down a blue print for understanding the foundation of the Temple and creation. This has been, for me, a multi- faceted jewel with breathtaking spiritual meaning. Dinah's years of research and study have give us the opportunity to glean from her work and unlock a treasure that G-d is revealing to this generation of worshippers who long for His presence.

ANNETTE GARCIA, GENERAL MANAGER
SON BROADCASTING NETWORK

The Temple Revealed in Creation: A Portrait of the Family

By Dinah Dye

Foundations in Torah Publishing

Unless otherwise noted, Scripture quotations are taken from the Complete Jewish Bible by David H. Stern. Copyright © 1998. All rights reserved. Used by permission of Messianic Jewish Publishers, 6120 Day Long Lane, Clarksville, MD 21029. www.messianicjewish.net.

ISBN 978-0-9972410-0-6

First Printing, 2016

Visit the author's website at
www.FoundationsInTorah.com

DEDICATION

This book is dedicated to my G-d and His Messiah, *Yeshua.* I sensed His presence every step of the way — leading and guiding me through all the various twists and turns of this book. He ministered to me when I struggled and poured out His Wisdom upon me, often in the dead of night, when I was stuck. To G-d be the glory forever!

To my husband, Michael, who was always confident I'd complete this book, even when I was not, and whose love and support made this even possible. Thank you from the bottom of my heart for never clipping my wings and for giving me the freedom to fly.

To my daughters, Hannah and Sarah, who never once doubted. You have given me the greatest treasure of all — the pure joy of my three grandchildren: Ya'el, Gavriella and Remy.

PSALM 27.4-6

Just one thing have I asked of Adonai;
Only this will I seek;
To live in the house of Adonai
All the days of my life,
To see the beauty of Adonai
And visit in His Temple.
For He will conceal me in His shelter
On the day of trouble,
He will hide me in the folds of his tent,
He will set me high on a rock.
Then my head will be lifted up
Above my surrounding foes,
And I will offer in His tent
Sacrifices with shouts of joy;
I will sing, sing praises to Adonai!

CONTENTS

ACKNOWLEDGMENTS

I would like to acknowledge and extend a big thank you to my editor, Sarah Hawkes Valente. She was my guiding light and my motivation throughout this entire project. She is a true treasure, and I'm so grateful for her. No matter how confusing my thought process, or how chaotic the wording, she always managed to turn it to magic.

Thank you, Tyler Dawn Rosenquist, for your attention to detail, your excellent suggestions, and, as you say, your "meddling" ways. Also thanks to David Farley for his formatting prowess.

A very special thank you goes to Joe Good for all these years of laying a solid foundation in temple studies upon which I could build.

Finally, thanks to my soul sisters, Bodie Thoene and Robin Hanley, for your love and encouragement. I couldn't be more delighted to have you as my "bookends" — to Robin for your masterful cover design and to Bodie who has been my inspiration for many years. Also to dear little Shalom, a child of astonishing spiritual vision, who was repeatedly heard saying, "Dinah Dye has the key to the Temple!" It was all the motivation I needed.

INTRODUCTION

The subject of the Temple usually generates a great deal of debate — peppered with lots of questions and sprinkled with more than a little controversy. Some view the Temple as a building that was destroyed in the first century but will be built again to fulfill the prophecies of Daniel and Revelation. Others think the Temple is irrelevant because *Yeshua's* (Jesus) sacrifice replaced it. Some are waiting for a new Temple to appear out of the heavens, while others are taking steps to build it here on earth. Some see the Temple in abstract and spiritual terms, while others see only a physical building. Those with no opinion have been content to leave the entire subject to the "experts." Ultimately, the question that should be asked is, "What is the relevance of the Temple for believers in *Yeshua* (Jesus) the Messiah?"

We are indeed fortunate that so many excellent resources have been translated into English from Hebrew, Greek, and Aramaic. These sources concentrate on the Temple's history, its physical design, its rituals and ceremonies, and its mechanics. However, there are no ancient sources that really explain the meaning of temple symbols. Extra-biblical sources from the Second Temple period include the same symbols found in the Bible, but their meaning is also shrouded in mystery. Where do we begin in deciphering them? Well, learning the Temple's design, structure, and function (through studying historical and archaeological sources as well as ancient culture and context) is an important place to start. This will help lay a solid foundation that will allow for a studied examination of the rich imagery and symbolism of the Temple world. I do believe the Temple is *the* framework and template for understanding Scripture.

I have spent more than the past 35 years connecting the Gospels and Epistles to their foundation in the Torah. Through my study, the big picture eventually emerged for me. I now see the Temple as the overlying structural blueprint for the entire Bible. Since I have a tendency to get bogged down in details, it was nice to finally see the larger pattern. When it comes to my study of Scripture, I have often considered myself to be an amateur forensic detective; I thrive on evaluating clues and identifying biblical patterns. Now I "see" the Temple everywhere — and in everything. Yes, we all have filters we use to study — I just happen to think the Temple filter is key.

The more symbols and idioms I uncovered, the more kept sprouting up all around me. I can now say with confidence that the Bible is filled with temple imagery and idioms: green pastures, the garden, dry ground, the vineyard, the couch, the forest, the threshing floor, the bird's nest, the sheepfold... Revelation is a classic example of a book that is bursting with metaphorical language related to the Temple. It is filled with symbols that were likely understood by first century Christians, but they are basically foreign to us. We cannot evaluate these symbols from our twenty-first century mindset. If we do, then locusts become helicopters, beasts with seven heads become modern-day geo-political states, and the Catholic Church becomes the whore of Babylon. Revelation is foremost an Ancient Near East (ANE) temple text filled with symbols and imagery that must be evaluated from a first-century perspective. We cannot make the text say what it does not say.

In this first volume, *The Temple Revealed in Creation: A Portrait of the Family*, I will lay a foundation from the standpoint of creation and introduce the spiritual nature of the Temple through a variety of topics: the Creation Covenant, the Holy of Holies, the concept of unity and separation, the Day of Atonement, and the meaning and purpose of Wisdom. In each chapter, I will present a fictional account (a Midrash) from the biblical narrative. (In the time of the Second Temple period, the Midrash was a popular method for communicating important concepts.) I will also incorporate an academic explanation of the material and conclude with a personal commentary. Future book titles include, *The Temple Revealed in the Garden*, *The Temple Revealed in the Days of Noah*, *The Temple Revealed in the Tents of the Patriarchs*, and so on. Available on my website, **Foundations in Torah**, are 30 minute videos that accompany each book volume and provide additional information on the topic presented.

My personal opinions on the Temple have been formed through my research in the Jewish and Christian extra-biblical sources of the Second Temple period, writings from the Ancient Near East world, and years of studying the Hebraic nature of the New Testament. Biblical quotes are from the *Complete Jewish Bible*, by David Stern, unless otherwise stated. This translation was chosen for its Hebrew flavor and not necessarily for its scholarly content. Some of the teachings and spiritual connections introduced in this book will be expounded upon in later volumes.

My purpose in writing this series is to help believers in *Yeshua* the Messiah recognize temple language and recover the spiritual meaning behind the biblical symbols the way first-century believers understood them. Studying the Temple can be compared to diving head-first into a powerful drama; it excites and inspires and causes a little palpitation of the heart. This is a deep well that will never run dry, and no one will ever be able to mine all the precious gems that can be found through temple studies. My ultimate hope, dear reader, is that you will enter the divine, supernatural world of the place of His Presence — and be forever changed.

PROLOGUE

*In the fifteenth day of the seventh month you are to
have a holy convocation…you are to observe a feast to
Adonai seven days…in addition to the regular burnt
offerings with its grain and drink offerings*
(Num. 29.12,16).

Darkness crept over the city of Jerusalem. The moon appeared above the horizon casting its silvery glow on the stone walls of the Temple buildings. It glimmered across the cold pavement of the Court of the Women where a large crowd had gathered. It was the last night of *Sukkot* (Feast of Tabernacles), and the excitement was palpable.

As the light from the moon intensified, four young priests-in-training, called "the flowers of Priesthood," climbed up four ladders which were propped against four large lamp stands that stood in the Women's Court. The young priests steadily scaled the ladders so as not to spill a drop of the pressed olive oil they carried in open pitchers. The olive oil was the fuel source for the great lamps. Once the young priests reached the large vats that were mounted on the lamp stands, they quickly poured the oil to light both the outer and inner lamps. Wicks for the outer lamps were made from the old trousers of the priests; wicks for the inner lamps were made from the trousers of the high priest himself. Once the wicks were lit, the night was ablaze; every corner and courtyard of Jerusalem was illuminated as though it were noonday.

The mood of the crowd was electric. The atmosphere in the Court of the Women had been supernaturally transformed. The men held burning torches and danced with reverent jubilation while Levitical priests played musical instruments with great exuberance and passion. The great scholars and sages of Israel were among those who had gathered in the courtyard. These men were well-known not only for their scholarship but also for their piety and character. Yet they participated joyfully in the celebration with hand clapping, foot stomping, and enthusiastic singing. An audible gasp rose from the crowd as *Rabbi Shimon Ben Gamliel* juggled eight torches at the same time without dropping even one. The men danced like King David danced before the Ark of the Covenant — leaping and spinning and whirling before the Lord.

Meanwhile, women and children who came to Jerusalem for the feast sat in the specially constructed raised balconies that lined the edge of the courtyard. As the women chatted together in barely audible tones, the children fidgeted impatiently in their seats and tried to suppress giggles as they watched their fathers dance and sing. Without warning, the crowd below erupted with shouts of, "Halleluyah! Praise the Lord from the heavens! Praise Him in the heights. Praise Him sun and moon; praise Him all bright stars. Praise Him the most exalted of the heavens and the waters that are above the heavens!" The chant from the crowd was followed by the sweet, melodious sounds of harps and lyres which echoed far and wide throughout the deep canyons surrounding Jerusalem. Every now and then, a quick blast from a ram's horn pierced the night. Tambourines and flutes, along with the occasional loud clash of cymbals, added to the drama.

In front of the bronze doors of the Nicanor Gate, and above the semi-circular stone stairway, the Levitical choir took their places on the platform. It was not unusual for them to sing from this elevated place; the choir sang from this spot when they accompanied the regular morning and evening offerings. But tonight was special. Tonight they sang the fifteen Songs of Ascent with intensified emotion in anticipation of the *Simcha Beit HaShoevah* (Rejoicing in the House of the Water Drawing). "I raise my eyes to the hills; where does my help come from? My help is from the Lord, Maker of heaven and earth," reverberated throughout the Temple complex.

After a long night of celebration, the first rays of the morning sun appeared in the eastern sky over the hills of Hebron. Though some had fallen asleep, many of the celebrants, now near exhaustion, continued dancing and singing. They were eager for the water drawing portion of the ceremony. A clear, high-pitched call from the Temple crier rang throughout the Temple precincts signaling the men of Israel, the Priests, and the Levites to prepare for the day's services.

Meanwhile, at the entrance to the Nicanor Gate, two young priests blew silver trumpets. Anticipation grew. The two priests moved slowly and deliberately down the semicircular steps. When they reached the tenth step, they stopped and blew the trumpets again. Once they reached the stone floor of the women's courtyard, they paused and blew the trumpets before crossing the pavement to the eastern gate. With the last blast, the crowd made their way onto the Temple Mount. Before making their descent to the Pool of *Shiloach* (Siloam), the worshippers pressed forward slightly then stopped abruptly. They turned back in unison to face the Holy Sanctuary. By this act, the crowd declared their worship of G-d in His throne room, the Holy of Holies, which was towards the west. Their forefathers had faced east, towards the sun, to worship.

They continued down from the Temple Mount, passing through the Huldah Gates to the underground twin passageway of the Double Gate with its unique Herodian features. Some in the crowd glanced up momentarily to appreciate the fine, decorative dome ceiling that had been meticulously carved in stone. Meanwhile, the high priest quickly passed through the Water Gate, so named for this ceremony, in order to join the crowd as they descended to the Pool of *Shiloach*. The night had indeed been a joyous one, but now their joy would increase as the worshippers witnessed the double ritual of the drawing of water from the pool and the pouring out of water on the great altar. Today's ceremony at the pool was particularly significant, as the high priest himself would be the one to draw the water.

As the high priest made his way down the broad steps of the plaza into the cool waters of the pool of *Shiloach*, the worshippers closed ranks behind him. Between the enormous Herodian columns, the crowd squeezed in tightly — each one eager for a better view. The Pool of *Shiloach* was uniquely situated in the shadow of the Holy Temple, and it received its water from the Gihon Spring: the water supply for the city of Jerusalem. A channel constructed along the eastern slope of the City of David had originally been built to irrigate King Solomon's garden. Later, however, King Hezekiah constructed a channel through solid rock — diverting the water inside the city walls in order to protect the vulnerable supply from foreign invaders. Now the pool, which had formed from the water in the channel, was the site of one of Israel's most important rituals: the water drawing.

The golden flask carried by the high priest shimmered in the early morning sunlight. As he scooped up the half-liter of pure water from the pool, the crowd nodded its collective approval and cheered loudly with delight. The multitudes then turned and followed the high priest back up the well-worn path to the Temple Mount; it was now time for the second part of the ritual that coincided with the daily morning offerings. All the while they sang the fifteen Songs of Ascent, "…I was glad when they said to me, The House of *Adonai*! Let's go! Our feet were already standing at your gates, Jerusalem."

As the boisterous crowd re-entered the Temple precincts,

passing again through the Water Gate, the priests standing on the steps began blowing the silver trumpets. The worshippers responded enthusiastically: "Therefore with joy shall you draw waters from the wells of salvation!" They followed closely behind the high priest as he entered the inner courtyard and ascended the large stone ramp of the great altar. He made his way to the altar where two attached silver bowls served as receptacles for the water libation as well as for wine from the morning offering.

Before pouring out the water, the high priest held up the golden flask for the entire crowd to see. It seemed a Sadducean priest who opposed the entire ceremony had recently poured the ceremonial water onto his feet instead of into the silver bowl for which it was meant. The crowd reacted strongly to this act of contempt, and they pelted the offending priest with their *etrogim* (large lemon-like fruit). On this day, however, the high priest poured out the portion of water in an attitude of thanksgiving — with gratitude to G-d for sending His Spirit to bring salvation and for providing rain to the crops and blessings to the nation.

One veteran priest who served as assistant to the high priest had also made his way up the ramp to the location of the bowls. He carried with him a silver vessel containing the wine for the daily libation. In perfect unison, the high priest and his assistant poured their libations into the two silver bowls. The bowl positioned eastward was for the wine while the bowl positioned westward was for the water. Since wine is somewhat thicker than water, the hole in the bottom of the east-facing bowl was marginally larger allowing water and wine to flow together.

From the bowl, the wine ran down into a special vat underneath the altar. Every seventy years, young priests would descend to this vat to collect the congealed wine which by then resembled dried rounds of pressed figs. The water, on the other hand, flowed through perpendicular shafts called "*shitin*" to an underground channel that joined the brook *Kidron*. From there, the water flowed into the *Gihon* River and down the valley to complete the cycle. According to the sages, the portion drawn from the *Shiloach* was returning to the waters of the *Gihon* Spring, called the fountain of living waters, and so back to the waters of creation. Legend told that in order to bring each country its power and assortment of fruit these shafts routed the water through a subterranean network of canals that issued from underneath the Temple Mount.

Once the water and the wine disappeared from view, the crowd let out a prolonged shout of *Hoshanna* (save us). With that, the official ceremony was over. Now they waited for the rains to come and water the crops — blessing the whole House of Israel with a bountiful final harvest.

CHAPTER ONE

WATER AND FIRE

In His goodness renews daily, perpetually,
the work of creation. How great are Your works,
HaShem, You make them all with wisdom,
the world is full of Your possessions.
(*Me'ir*: Benediction for the *Shema*)

In the fall of 2014, at *Sukkot* (Feast of Tabernacles), hundreds of orthodox Jews who were led by the Temple Institute gathered in the archaeological park of the City of David. History was being made. The crowd was there to re-enact the *Simcha Beit HaShoevah*, or the Rejoicing in the House of the Water Drawing, for the first time in nearly 2000 years. After descending to the Pool of *Shiloach* (Siloam), their ranks swelled to over a thousand as the procession made its way back up to the old city of Jerusalem. Among the participants was a small group from New Mexico who had happened upon the entire event and was thrilled at their good fortune.

The crowd eventually made its way to the main square of the Old City in front of the beautiful Hurva synagogue. There, two young men dressed in white, priestly garments poured the water and wine into the silver cups resting on the makeshift, cinderblock altar. This modern-day water drawing ceremony may not have been clothed in the majesty and splendor of the original celebration in the Temple, but the enthusiasm and the sense of destiny emanating from the crowd more than made up for that. In fact, many now believe that the re-enactment signaled the end of the age, the rebuilding of the Temple, and the return of the Messiah!

Why should we pay so much attention to the water drawing? This ceremony is a great example of a "creation renewal" ritual. The idea of "creation renewal" is key in understanding the connection between the Holy Temple and the creation of the world: the main message for this book. "The creation" and "the Temple" are synonymous terms, so the Temple rituals and ceremonies are not only critical components of the Temple but are an integral part of the first covenant established by G-d: the Creation Covenant. To restore this covenant is to rebuild the Temple and to re-enact the rituals. Covenant concepts such as light and water, the union of male and female elements, Wisdom and the ministry of the Holy Spirit, and the restoration of the unity of the Holy of Holies through repentance are just some of the topics that need to be addressed.

The water drawing ceremony was certainly one of Israel's most joyous celebrations during the Second Temple period. Unfortunately, by that time, the meaning of the service had been largely forgotten. The ritual is not mentioned in the *Tanakh* (OT); although, according to the sages, there *is* a veiled reference to it in the account of the libation offerings required for *Sukkot* (Num. 29.17-33). While it remains unclear whether the water drawing ceremony was ever performed in Solomon's Temple, the ceremony was known as a renewal ritual in memory of the creation. Therefore, when *Yeshua*

(Jesus) spoke to his disciples on the last day of *Sukkot* and said, "Rivers of living water will flow," (Jn. 7.37-39) it is likely he was imparting revelation about the restoration of creation.

When the water drawn from the Pool of *Shiloach* (meaning "sent") was poured onto the altar, it inevitably returned to the waters of creation: the *Gihon* Spring. A copper laver, used for ritual washing in the Temple, was filled with water drawn from the *Gihon* as well. The laver, called the "sea," was a large kettle-like vessel with spigots. Each day, the priests would wash their hands and feet before beginning the morning services and entering the Temple building. The laver represented "the primeval waters in ritual" because the courtyard surrounding the laver represented "the sea surrounding the stable earth" (Barker 2008: 65). According to Numbers *Rabbah* (13.19), "the court surrounds the Temple just as the sea surrounds the world." The Book of Revelation (4.6) describes the "sea of glass like crystal surrounding the heavenly throne." The water originating from under the Temple Mount that was used for these Temple ceremonies was known as both the *waters of creation* and the *fountain of living water*: the *Gihon*.

What did the water drawing ceremony signify for the believers of the first century? We can only speculate, but a verse in the Book of Enoch connects water to Wisdom and the Spirit, "Wisdom is poured out like water," and describes the Elect One as being filled with "the spirit of Wisdom, the spirit which gives insight, and the spirit of understanding and of might" (1 Enoch 49.1,3). (The Book of Enoch is an important work particularly for its historical and religious development in Judaism dating back from 200 BCE to 100 CE. This book is part of the Pseudepigrapha, Jewish writings whose authors used a pseudonym, and is considered a non-canonical work that was ascribed to Enoch, the great-grandfather of Noah. The book was familiar to the NT writers, was quoted in Jude 1.14.15, and was attributed to the earlier Chasids and then later the Pharisees. It was originally written partly in Aramaic and partly in Hebrew in five sections that paralleled the five books of the Torah as well as other works such as the Psalms.)

Perhaps when *Yeshua* said, "Whoever is thirsty let him come to me and drink," or when he spoke of "rivers of living waters" flowing from "his innermost being" (Jn. 7.37), he was referring to the return of Wisdom to the Holy of Holies. Interestingly, his comments were made in the Holy Temple in Jerusalem on the last day of *Sukkot*, called *Hoshanah Rabbah*: the Day of the Great Salvation. "Now he said this about the Spirit, whom those who trusted in him were to receive later" (Jn. 7.39). Perhaps *Yeshua* was also declaring that the Spirit, as the embodiment of Wisdom, would once again flow like rivers of living water. The Book of Enoch suggests wisdom as water flows from the fountain of living water inside the Holy of Holies:

> And in that place I saw the fountain of righteousness which was inexhaustible: And around it were many fountains of wisdom: And all the thirsty drank of them, and were filled with wisdom, and their dwellings were with the righteous and holy and elect. And at that hour that Son of Man was named in the presence of the Lord of Spirits, and his name before the Head of Days.
>
> (1 ENOCH 48.1,2)

In the book of Proverbs, Wisdom is personified as a wife who built herself a house by carving seven pillars (Prov. 9.1). She is compared to streams of water flowing into the streets and to a fountain of fresh water that brings life and joy (Prov. 5.15-18). Wisdom is linked to the water of the Spirit that quenches thirst.

> The Spirit and the Bride say, "Come!" Let him who hears say, "Come!" And let anyone who thirsts come let anyone who wishes, take the water of life free of charge.
>
> (REV. 22.17)

British scholar Margaret Barker shares another aspect of Wisdom connected to the Creation Covenant:

> Wisdom was the tree of life whose fruit gave wisdom, whose leaves were for healing and whose oil was used for anointing, to open eyes...and she was the bond who held all things in harmony. She was, in effect, the Creation Covenant described sometimes as the Spirit and sometimes as righteousness.
>
> (BARKER 2010: 250)

The relationship between Wisdom and the Spirit (discussed in chapter 5) and the ritual water pouring is first hinted at in Genesis. We are told the Spirit of G-d (the Divine Presence) hovered over the face of the waters (1.2). The sages believed that, "In the beginning, before creation, the world was but water in water" (Genesis *Rabbah* 5.2). Then, G-d separated the waters. The male waters above were divided from the female waters below; the female waters were called *tehom* (deep). Ancient tradition had it that when the two waters were forced apart they wept over their desire to be reunited.

> Receive us, you are the creation of the Holy One, blessed be He and we are his envoys. Immediately they received them...like unto this female that opens before the male.
>
> (GENESIS *Rabbah* 13)

According to legend, once water from the golden vessel was poured onto the altar, into the silver bowl, it ran down through shafts to meet the waters of the deep. This caused the lower waters to rise up to meet the waters above, and so their union created new life. Rabbi *Yehudah* said, "All that the Holy One, blessed be He, created in His world He created male and female" (BT *Baba Batra* 74b). Even floods were considered the result of the union between male and female waters. In the ANE (Ancient Near East), when the Tigris and Euphrates flooded each year to the benefit of the crops, it was understood that this flooding represented the union between male and female deities (Patai 1947). Rabbi *Abahu* referred to the upper waters as a bridegroom and the lower waters as a bride. His analogy was illustrated when the rains came at *Sukkot*; the waters above united with the waters below like a groom with his bride in their *Sukkah* (booth).

Creation could be defined, then, as the reuniting of male and female elements in order for two to become one house and to produce life. The Creation Covenant is essentially a covenant related to betrothal and marriage. This is temple building activity, for to build a temple was to build a house and family. Temple services and ceremonies, which were re-enactments of creation, strengthened the bonds of this covenant.

> The biblical worldview is a vision of the unity of all things, and how the visible material world relates to another dimension of existence that unites all things into one divinely ordained system known as the eternal covenant, the Creation Covenant.
>
> (BARKER 2010: 19)

Hosea cements this picture for us when he reveals there is a *day* coming — a day of the unity of all things — when the Creation Covenant, as a betrothal ritual, is restored:

> When That Day comes I will make a covenant for them with the wild animals, the birds in the air and the creeping things of the earth. I will break bow and sword, sweep battle from the land and make them lie down securely. I will betroth you to me forever; yes, I will betroth you to me in righteousness, in justice, in grace and in compassion; I will betroth you to me in faithfulness, and you will know

Adonai. When That Day comes, I will answer, says *Adonai*
I will answer the sky and it will answer the earth.

(HOS. 2.20-23)

The Creation Covenant

*And Mount Sinai was wrapped in smoke, because the LORD
descended upon it in fire; and the smoke of it went up like the
smoke of a kiln, and the whole mountain quaked greatly.*

(EX. 19.18 RSV)

The story of *Avram* and the covenant between the parts is rich
in meaning and symbolism. The burning torch and smoking
furnace that passed between the parts of the severed animals
confirmed the Creation Covenant between *Avram* and G-d.
In the Bible, the narrative contains few details. The following
fictional portrayal is an example of a *midrashic* legend which
was popular during the Second Temple period and well into
the Talmudic era. A Midrash is a method of biblical interpretation that fills in the gaps of the narrative and focuses on
events and characters instead of moral and legal teachings:

The day was unseasonably warm. *Avram* left the protective
shade of his tent and with sweat dripping from his forehead
made his way to the slaughtering area of his camp — it was
time to slay the regular afternoon burnt offering. He was
startled by the sound of a violent, rushing wind that seemed
all at once to consume him. *Avram* worried the wind might
damage the camp, but the howling stopped just as abruptly
as it had started. He breathed a sigh of relief as he glanced
knowingly toward the heavens. His seed would outnumber
the stars in the sky; that was the promise G-d had made him.

Avram steadied the lamb and began the ritual slaughtering.
Although this task was done twice daily, today was different.
Avram cut the animals into halves only instead of the usual

nine parts. He placed the halves on the ground, opposite one another, leaving room between them for a path. The blood from the animals spread out in every direction. Some seeped into the ground leaving behind a bright, red stain. The image reminded *Avram* of his ancestor, Adam, the high priest of the garden in Eden. The Hebrew word for Adam came from *Adamah*, meaning "red earth," and from *dam*, meaning "blood."

As the day waned, and darkness descended over the camp, the tinny smell of blood attracted a small wake of vultures who began to attack the carcasses. *Avram* waved furiously at them, driving them away; once they had gone, he returned to his tent where he sat engulfed in thick darkness. *Avram* felt as if he'd returned to those first moments of creation when everything was empty, void, and utterly black. As he fell into a deep sleep, he heard the distinctive voice of the Divine Presence: "This land where you have pitched your tent belongs to you and your seed, forever." It was though he had entered the realm of the Holy of Holies: the place of the oracle of G-d.

Suddenly, through the darkness, *Avram* became aware of a blinding light just outside the tent opening. It caused *Avram* to reflect on the first light of creation. He let out a gasp when he saw the source: a smoking furnace and a torch of fire passing between the animals he had cut in half. *Avram* knew this was the Divine Presence. The dark smoke from the furnace filled the camp and slowly crept inside *Avram's* tent. He remembered the stories he had heard from the ancients, the high priests of old, who entered the Holy of Holies one day each year to make atonement for the people. *Avram* recognized the service of the blood and the incense. He knew these things were related to atonement — that they were part of a resto- ration ritual intended to re-establish the Creation Covenant which had been broken in the garden. He knew the smoke from the fiery coals, on which the *ketoret* (incense) was placed, brought a heavenly fragrance that would dispel the thick dark- ness and cause the foul smell of the blood to dissipate. *Avram* understood that the sweet smell of the *ketoret* empowered the human soul to return to the One True G-d. Repentance was *the* sign that the "Creation Covenant," which had been broken through disobedience, was now repaired — that the way into the Holy of Holies was unobstructed. The covenant sealed that day meant *Avram's* seed would someday find permanent rest in the land G-d promised. *Avram* understood this.

✧   ✧   ✧

Understanding covenants is paramount to understanding the Bible. Most Christians are familiar with the Abrahamic, the Mosaic, and the Davidic covenants. And, of course, Christians acknowledge the *Brit Chadasha*, the New or Renewed Covenant (NT), which is the foundation for our faith in Messiah *Yeshua*. But few understand or even recognize the Creation Covenant. According to Margaret Barker, the Creation Covenant was also called the "everlasting covenant" or the "covenant of peace" (2010: 122). She further explains that the Creation Covenant was a conditional covenant whereby repentance would restore the broken bonds: "a broken Creation Covenant brought the wrath and so repairing the breach in the covenant was called atonement" (2010: 123). Irenaeus stated, "The covenant renewed in the New Testament was fundamentally the Creation Covenant." Restoring the covenant first required an act of atonement. This is *Yeshua's* blood of the "New Covenant." The blood and incense services that took place inside the Holy of Holies on *Yom Kippur* (Day of Atonement) were atonement rituals. Symbolically, these rituals prevented the destructive consequences of wrath and judgment.

The Creation Covenant is not specifically named in the Bible; it is hidden in the Hebrew letters of the first word, *Beresheet*: in the beginning. Two Hebrew words form the word *Beresheet*: *brit*, meaning "covenant," and *esh*, meaning "fire." The Creation Covenant was the *Covenant of Fire*. "When G-d created the world, it was created only through a covenant" (Zohar I, 89a). Although *brit* is translated "to cut," it really means "joining" together two halves. A covenant, therefore, describes a relationship in which two join together to become one. A marriage covenant is an example of the "covenant of fire." The Hebrew word for man, *eish*, and woman, *eishah*, are both formed from the word for fire: *esh*. An animal cut in two, *brit*, was likened to the woman being "cut" from the man. Creation restored meant G-d was entering into a covenantal relationship with His creation by joining together male and female to become one house. The Covenant of Fire, which sealed the unity between husband and wife, was ratified in the inner chamber of the Holy of Holies between G-d, the husband and Israel, the wife. Enoch described the Holy of Holies as a *house of fire* (1 Enoch 71.5,6).

In the ancient world, a covenant was an agreement between two parties. Certain conditions applied under which each party promised something to the other. A covenant was instituted by offering a fatted animal that was cut in half. As the two parties passed between the halves of the animal, they cemented their union by agreeing to fulfill the terms of their covenant. If one party failed to satisfy their obligations, the other party was released from the contract. When a covenant was broken, the bond between the two parties was also broken. This resulted in complete collapse of the agreement. The covenant provided protection; once broken, it had to be fixed or wrath and judgment followed. Again, the services of blood and incense on the Day of Atonement were ritual re-enactments that restored the collapsed Creation Covenant to its original state.

The Temple ritual for the Day of Atonement must have expressed the restoration of the original state...atonement concerned the renewal of the creation and so was at the heart of the Christian message.

(BARKER 2010: 92)

The setting for the *Brit Esh*, the "Covenant of Fire," was the Holy of Holies: the inner sanctum of the Temple. The Holy of Holies was called the *debir*, meaning oracle, where G-d spoke to His high priests and communicated things beyond the physical world of men. When G-d spoke, His Word resembled tongues of fire. In another passage, Enoch describes heaven as a great house surrounded by tongues of fire:

> And I beheld a vision...there was a second house, greater than the former...and it was built of flames of fire...and its floor was of fire, and above it were lightnings and the path of the stars, and its ceiling also was flaming fire. And I looked and saw therein a lofty throne: its appearance was as crystal, and the wheels thereof as the shining sun, and there was the vision of cherubim. And from underneath the throne came streams of flaming fire so that I could not look thereon. And the Great Glory sat thereon, and His raiment shone more brightly than the sun...the flaming fire was round about Him and a great fire stood before Him.
>
> (1 ENOCH 14.15-22)

Picture Moses on Mount Sinai receiving the Torah in the form of tongues of fire. The Bible describes Mount Sinai engulfed in smoke because G-d had descended upon the mountain in fire. The smoke ascended like the smoke of the furnace. The top of the mountain represented the inner sanctum of the Temple.

> Moses went up onto the mountain and the cloud covered the mountain. The glory of *Adonai* stayed on Mount Sinai and the cloud covered it for six days. On the seventh day he called to Moses out of the cloud. To the people of Israel the glory of *Adonai* looked like a raging fire on top of the mountain.
>
> (EX. 24.15-17)

It's not hard to see the pattern of the creation week emerge or Moses in his role as high priest in the Holy of Holies. The seventh day in this passage parallels the *Shabbat* (Sabbath) of creation. The time frame is a High Sabbath during the feast of *Shavuot* (Feast of Weeks or Pentecost). Later, the rabbis would connect *Shavuot* with the receiving of the Torah of Moses (the Pentateuch or first five books of the Bible). In this instance, the Torah appeared as tongues of fire coming out from the inner sanctum, the throne room of G-d's Holy Temple, just as Enoch described.

The *Covenant of Fire* functioned in the context of the Temple. This enhances our understanding of the second chapter of the book of Acts. The believers gathered in "one place" — a direct reference to the Temple. A sound like the roar of a violent wind filled the House. Notice, it is a *sound* that filled the house — not a substance. Then they saw tongues of fire. Although Scripture says the people were sitting, they could not have been sitting in the Temple building or the inner courtyard. Only a king descended from David could sit there. It is likely they sat in the Court of the Women where the four great lamps were erected for the festival of *Sukkot*. It was there that tongues of fire rested on each one of them. The "words" they spoke originated from G-d's oracle — the Holy of Holies in heaven — where the Ark of the Covenant sat with the stone tablets inside. It was the hour of the regular morning altar service and prayer. Luke quotes the prophet Joel, "I will pour out from my Spirit on everyone," suggesting Wisdom being poured out like water and fire. *Yeshua* had ascended to heaven and performed the services of the high priest — applying his blood to the altar and the incense to the burning coals. The Creation Covenant was restored, and the Kingdom of Heaven began to spread from the Holy of Holies to the uttermost parts of the world.

In the Beginning a House

> But in the last days it shall come to pass, that the mountain of the House of the Lord shall be established in the top of the mountains, and it shall be exalted above the hills; and people shall flow to it. And many nations shall come, and say, 'Come, and let us go up to the mountain of the Lord, and to the House of the G-d of Ya'akov; and He will teach us of His ways, and we will walk in His paths; for Torah shall go forth from Zion, and the word of the Lord from Jerusalem.
>
> (MICAH 4.1-2 KJV)

Jacob's journey to Bethel and his vision of the ladder standing between heaven and earth is one of the Bible's best-known stories. The following fictional vignette brings to life Jacob's journey to the mountain and his encounter with G-d. Both temples would eventually be built on the site where he visited:

Ya'acov (Jacob) left the comfort of his home in *Beersheva* (Beersheba). He traveled to Charan (Haran) to secure a bride from among his Great Uncle Laban's clan. Rebecca, his mother, desired that her son marry and build a house from among her own people. She was also concerned for her favorite son's safety, because his brother, *Esav*, was about to come against him. Since the journey to Charan was a strenuous one, *Ya'acov* detoured along the way to camp at a secluded spot near the city of Jerusalem. He'd heard stories from his grandfather, *Avraham*, and his father, *Itzchak* (Isaac), about a hidden place where G-d had appeared to them.

Traveling with only his livestock as companions, *Ya'acov* made his way northward towards the mountains of Jerusalem. As he drew near, he stopped to admire the view from the southern summit. From behind a cloud, the sun's rays poked through like beams of light casting a golden glow on the mountain peak where he was headed. He knew this was "the place." As he reached the crest, the setting sun brushed the sky with a rose-colored hue. Tired, hungry, and nearly spent from the long day, *Ya'acov* surveyed the area for a grassy spot on which to erect his tent. He found only a large outcropping, just below the peak, so he pitched his tent over the gently sloping rock. *Ya'acov* spotted a somewhat crude, stone altar to sacrifice his lamb for the evening's burnt offering, and then he noticed a small brook bubbling from underneath the rock. He took a long drink from the crystal clear water, and he washed his hands and feet before entering his tent — as priests before him had done. He praised G-d for his good fortune, remembering what his grandfather had said about "the place": "Underneath this stone was hidden the source of all springs and fountains from which the world drinks its water."

Before entering the tent, *Ya'acov* had taken twelve stones from the altar of burnt offering to arrange them around his head for protection. Somehow, miraculously, the twelve stones fused into one large stone as the last glimmer of light vanished from the sky. *Avraham* had come to this very same spot, many years before, to offer *Itzchak* on the same altar. *Ya'acov* remembered the story. G-d intervened, and *Avraham* found a ram, caught in a thicket, to offer as a substitute for *Ya'acov's* dad. His grandfather had told him the name of this special place. He'd called it, "On this mountain the Lord will be seen." It seemed to *Ya'acov* that "the place" was like a Holy House because the Divine Presence was there.

Thick darkness, reminiscent of creation, settled on the camp as *Ya'acov* fell into a deep sleep. He had a most curious dream. He saw a ramp set toward the ground with its top extended to heaven; angels ascended and descended on it. *Avraham* had told *Ya'acov* stories about temple life in Ur. The locals had helped the King of Ur build a giant ziggurat (stepped pyramid altar) for the Sumerian moon god, Nanna. The outer stairway of the ziggurat enabled Nanna to ascend and descend from heaven so his subjects could feed him. On one occasion after descending, he took his consort, Ningal, into the inner sanctum of his temple to consummate their marriage in order to produce god-like offspring.

Despite the ladder to heaven, *Ya'acov* knew this mountain sanctuary was different from those temples in the east. The altar of burnt offering in the Temple would be *the* contact point between man and the One True G-d. The rock where *Ya'acov* laid his head would become the future site of the Holy of Holies from which *Ya'acov's* seed would become the Sons of G-d.

> He [Jacob] took twelve stones, saying: 'The Holy One, blessed be He, has decreed that twelve tribes should spring forth. Now neither Abraham nor Isaac has produced them. If these twelve stones cleave to one another, then I know that I will produce the twelve tribes.' When therefore the twelve stones united, he knew that he was to produce the twelve tribes.
>
> R. *Judah*

In his dream, *Ya'acov* saw a blazing fire encircle the rock where he was sleeping. It was as though the power of G-d had completely overshadowed him — as if the Divine Presence literally seared His image into *Ya'acov's* body. The imprint left on the rock was that of a house in the shape of a man. Then *Ya'acov* heard the Divine Presence speak in thundering tones saying, "I am *Adonai*, G-d of *Avraham* your father, and G-d of *Itzchak*, the ground which you are lying upon, to you I will give it to your descendants." *Ya'acov*, as yet unmarried, now knew for sure the foundation for his house would be in "this place" and that his seed would spread to the four corners of the earth.

Ya'acov rose early the next morning, and he took the one stone that had come from twelve. He set it up as a pillar in the entrance of his tent to confirm a special covenant with G-d. It seemed to *Ya'acov* the stone was alive in this holy place. He anointed the rock with specially pressed olive oil, and he recited a blessing. *Surely*, he thought, *this is the place of the Holy of*

Holies, and I am confirming the "Covenant of Fire" with this oil of anointing. The living stone that had been taken from the altar of G-d reminded *Ya'acov* that one day a high priest, of the order of *Melchizedek,* would enter the Holy of Holies. There he would cover the sins of his entire house so that they could live forever. *Ya'acov* shook his head, very unsettled in his thoughts. He knew G-d was with him, so he renamed the place *Bethel (Beit El)*, House of G-d. "At the level of divinity the house symbolizes the purpose of all reality: to become a dwelling place below for the manifestation of G-d's presence" (Ginsburgh 1991: 46). "Not as Abraham who called [the Temple] a mountain…nor as Isaac who called it a field…but as Jacob who called it a house" (BT *Pesachim* 88a).

✡   ✡   ✡

ANE (Ancient Near East) scholars suggest that "in the beginning" or *beresheet* (the first word of the Bible) encompasses the entire seven-day creation week. "In the beginning" does not signify the first item in a sequence of events — nor does it mean something that happened before everything else. "In the beginning" *was* the completed creation week, and the phrase is synonymous with temple building and dedication rituals. The first letter of *beresheet* is *beit* which means "house" in the pictographic language. The letter *beit* is enlarged in a Torah scroll, and it has a numerical value of two. "Two" and "house" both indicate some type of separation or division. Separation, as we will see in chapter three, defines the act of creation. Creation is a process of first separating out pairs of elements in order to join them together as one. The building of houses or temples typifies the act of creation as well as a covenant confirming the union between two parties.

The ancient sages explained that G-d chose the letter *beit* for His house/Temple in order to reveal Himself in the natural world while remaining hidden in the eternal world. The enlarged letter *beit*, however, was a puzzle to them. "Why," they asked, did G-d choose the letter beit over the letter aleph — which is the first letter of the Hebrew alphabet and which represents G-d Himself?" A *Midrash* explains how the letter *beit* was chosen:

> The Midrash relates that all of the twenty-two letters of the Hebrew alphabet were inscribed on G-d's crown: When He was about to create the world, they [the letters] descended and assembled before Him, each one requesting that it be used for the Creation. First, the *tav* made its claim, then the *shin* and so on. Finally the *beit* came forward and said, 'Let the world be created with me, because all beings will use me to bless G-d.' G-d immediately accepted this claim and said, 'So shall the Creation begin.'
>
> (MUNK 1983: 57)

A letter is generally given its meaning based on the first time it is used in a root word. In this instance, the second word of the Bible, *barah* (to create), is the first time the letter *beit* is used in this way. The meaning of *beit*, "a house," is then related to *barah*, "to create." These are essentially interchangeable concepts, and so a house/temple is synonymous with creation.

Beresheet can also be re-arranged to form a variety of phrases related to the house. For example, *beit rosh* means "the house is head", and *barah shtei* means "he made two." This suggests the house/Temple is the head of all things and made from the union of two. A husband and wife form a house to protect and to provide for their seed and to bring stability to the family and to the tribal community. In Hebrew thinking, a man's wife is called his house even though "house" is a masculine noun. Seven days before Yom Kippur, the high priest was separated from his house, and another wife was prepared for him in case the first one died: "and he shall make atonement for himself and for his house, his house — this is his wife" (Mishnah *Yoma* 1.1). The second wife would become "his house" if the first died. The high priest could not enter the Holy of Holies on behalf of the nation unless he first atoned for himself and his wife.

Temples in the ANE (Ancient Near East) were generally constructed from stone blocks. *Aven,* the Hebrew word for stone, is formed from two words: *Av* (father) and *ben* (son). *Ben* is also the root of the verb *banah* which means "to build." Houses in the ancient world were established through the sons of the family. In the desert, new panels were added to the family tent when sons were born, but it was the women who were responsible for stitching the panels into the tent as well as taking down and putting up the tent. In effect, women built the house. This is why *Ya'acov's* two wives, Rachel and Leah, plus his two concubines were considered the builders of the House of Israel (Ruth 4.11). The walls of the Tabernacle, for example, were made of cloth woven by women. This theme is best expressed in Proverbs 31 which describes the woman of valor who procures wool and flax and works with eager hands to build a home. This woman, who is clothed in fine linen and purple, is also clothed in strength and dignity and is representative of the Temple: G-d's heavenly House. "When a man is at home, the foundation of his house is the wife for it is on account of her that the Divine Presence departs not from the house" (Zohar I, 50a).

Ultimately, every human family is meant to mirror creation through temple building activity. The work of creation, or "house building," is clearly seen in the context of marriage whereby the union of husband and wife produce offspring generation after generation. "In His goodness He renews daily, perpetually, the work of creation" (From the prayer *La'el,* a *Shema* benediction). Every home is to be a sanctuary for those dwelling inside and function like *the* creation Temple established by G-d.

The House Today

The difficulty modern believers have in seeing temple imagery reminds me of the sinking of the Titanic. As a child I developed an enduring fascination for Titanic's story. I read nearly everything I could find on the subject; I wanted to understand what really happened that night. To me, it was a cold case murder mystery waiting to be solved. I was excited when oceanographer and former naval intelligence officer Robert Ballard discovered the Titanic off the coast of Newfoundland in 1985.

Over the last 103 plus years, many theories had been offered up to explain the events that led to the Titanic's sinking. Years of speculation were finally put to rest when Tim Maltin, British author and historian, uncovered the real story after many, many hours of investigation. Today he is one of the world's leading experts on the Titanic and is the author of three books on the subject.

After combing through ships' logs, weather records, and thousands of first-hand accounts, Maltin uncovered what happened that fateful night. Eyewitnesses had all reported amazingly calm seas and a crystal clear, starry night — beyond anything they'd ever seen. The horizon looked as though it literally blended into the sky. As the ship sailed south, an "eerie haze" appeared that Titanic never seemed to reach. A cold front moved in quickly as she sailed from the warm waters of the Gulf Stream to the frigid waters of the Labrador Current. Tim Maltin recognized these signs as a thermal inversion whereby cold air becomes trapped under warm air. Atmospheric conditions were perfect for a super refraction (light bending) event that would create many optical illusions that night. In maritime circles, this phenomenon is known as a "cold water mirage." This mirage explains why the crew was unable to see the iceberg in time. It was hidden within the "eerie haze" under a false horizon.

For twenty-first-century students of the Bible, the world of the Temple is much like an iceberg that has been hidden in an "eerie haze." The mirage is our post-modern, western way of thinking with its heavy emphasis on the scientific over the mythological. But to the ancient world, the people to whom the Bible was actually written, perception was very different. They recognized that the world of the Temple existed outside of time and space. We call it *eternity*. Modern scholarship, almost exclusively, focuses on the Bible as a record of history. Mysterious topics such as the creation of the world end up in political arguments over dating, chronology, and material origins. But the ancients saw creation as a cosmic Temple that existed in the mythical (eternal) world outside of time. They viewed the cosmos (ordered universe) as G-d's sacred space and creation as His Temple.

To the ancient world, temple building, creation, and the cosmos were essentially the same, and they were modeled after G-d's image. According to ANE scholar Victor Hurowitz, creation was the act of building, and the Creator was the wise, knowledgeable, and discerning architect. Temple/house building activity is best expressed through the unifying of male and female elements. This pattern is found all through the creation week — heaven and earth, day and night, waters above and below, earth and sea, light and dark, Adam and Eve (each of these Hebrew pairs contains a masculine and feminine noun). When male and female elements join together, they form a house. Every human family is, therefore, a temple in miniature created in the image of G-d. A house/temple is defined as a husband and wife who together produce new life. The purpose of the family is to create new life, preserve it, and bring order and stability to the universe. Temples in the ANE provided that stability to the community in which they were built.

The Temple/house was conceived in the mind of G-d. The blueprint for a strong family is based upon obedience to the first commandment, "Be fruitful and multiply and fill the earth" (Gen. 1.22,28). The creation story portrays building a house and then filling it. Temple building accounts in the ANE describe how the gods filled their houses with wealth and riches and all kinds of good things. And so, like a temple, the cosmos was *filled* with heavenly bodies, the earth was *filled* with life-giving seed to make it fruitful, the heavenly Temple was *filled* with G-d's glory, the garden was *filled* with life-giving trees, and Noah's ark was *filled* with animals and a family. King Solomon filled his house with G-d's wisdom in order to provide the kingdom with the proper administration of justice and righteousness. This likely explains the real meaning of being "filled" with the Holy Spirit. This is temple language that describes G-d's community as a "temple" where the Holy Spirit (Wisdom) dwells. That temple should be filled with all good things — love, joy, peace, patience, kindness, goodness, faithfulness, gentleness and self-control. The glory of G-d filling the earth and the human family filling society expresses this ideal.

G-d is the author of order, and He gives us the privilege of being fruitful and multiplying and filling His house. Unfortunately, today's family is under tremendous pressure from the culture at large. The institution of marriage is being torn apart. The foundations are crumbling under the weight of sin and disobedience, and the created order is collapsing as natural laws are continually violated. The breakdown of the family is nothing new, however. The Bible reveals the unhealthy spiritual condition of the House of Israel throughout its history. There was plenty of "family dysfunction" to go around. Our function in the Kingdom is to populate the world with seed (the word of G-d) without limitation or restriction. His Kingdom is the center of the ordered world where He preserves, protects, and creates life — and where function is realized.

Disorder and brokenness in the world (cosmos) are the result of human sin and the fall. We have much work to do to repair the family. I believe restoring families is critical not only for the culture and society but for the restoration of creation itself. Every family that is healed puts the kingdom of darkness on notice that the Creation Covenant is being renewed and the house of G-d restored. Unity is the glorious fruit. This is especially true for the Body of Messiah which is very fractured today. *Yeshua* spoke of unity in the context of his body which he described as a temple (Jn. 2.21).

> You have built on the foundation of the emissaries and the prophets, with the cornerstone being *Yeshua* the Messiah himself. In union with him the whole building is held together, and it is growing into a Holy Temple in union with the Lord. Yes, in union with him, you yourselves are being built together into a spiritual dwelling-place for G-d!
>
> (EPH. 2.20-22)

Studying the function, design, services, and ceremonies of the Temple will help bring unity to the Body of Messiah. Unity is not something we can accomplish in our own strength, but when we seek to *know* Him and the power of *Yeshua's* resurrection, He will reveal Himself in the place of His Presence. Certainly we long for Him to dwell in our midst. One commentary (Midrash *Tanhuma*) even suggests that learning the Temple in the Bible is as great as building it, and that those who study the Temple — when they are immersed in it — will be rewarded. The reward: He will give us credit for building His House.

CHAPTER TWO

HEAVEN AND SEA

You spread out the heavens like a curtain,
you laid the beams of your palace on the water...
you fixed the earth on its foundations never to be
moved. You covered it with the deep like a garment;
the waters stood above the mountains.
(Ps. 104.3,5,6)

The earth is Adonai's, with all that is in it, the world
and those who live there; for he set its foundations on
the seas and established it on the rivers.
(Ps. 24.1,2)

The mythological world of gods and goddesses is far removed from today's modern, secular life. The following vignette presents an imaginary account of the creation of the world from the perspective of the ancient Sumerian god, Enki, of Akkadian and Babylonian myth traditions:

Enki folded his arms, sat back in his chair, and congratulated himself on a job well done. His throne was now the recognized center of the universe. To reign as king of the cosmos was the mission handed him by his father, Enlil, sovereign over all the gods. Enki's father blessed him with wisdom, knowledge and understanding to create the universe, and he commissioned him to rule both the heavens above and the raging waters below.

Enki had finally defeated the powers of chaos: the watery abyss which had risen up against his authority. If the abyss had been victorious, it would have wiped his entire household from existence. Sea monsters lurked in the depths — waiting for their chance to destroy the cosmos. Enki knew the abyss by name; she was Tiamat, the primordial goddess of the ocean. Tiamat was famous for her relentless attacks against the gods and for bringing chaos to the burgeoning cosmos. She was frequently referred to as the "glistening one" — for her skin glowed with a radiant and unmatched beauty. In reality, she was the goddess who embodied wickedness, chaos, and disorder. Tiamat's desire was to overthrow the cosmos and replace it with her own primeval waters. Had Enki not stepped in, she would have triumphed. Fortunately, Enki had trained his son, Marduk, for the task of dislodging Tiamat from the realm of the fresh waters above. Tiamat was one with her husband, Apsu, who was the fresh waters. Once Marduk captured her, he sliced her in half. He sent Apsu to the heavens above and relegated Tiamat to the underworld below.

Enki savored his sweet victory — especially the accolades of the gods. The waters of chaos and turmoil had been completely subdued, and Tiamat's plan to rule the cosmos had been utterly and permanently thwarted. The universe now belonged solely to Enki who was the great water god and "Lord over the Abyss." Enki stabilized the cosmos by affixing a bolt to prevent Tiamat's waters from expanding past their boundary. To preserve the separation between Apsu and Tiamat, the fresh waters above from the salt waters below, Enki fashioned a flat, earthen-colored disc which he caused to float between the two. The disc was the primordial mound that would soon become the mountain on which he would build his earthly temple in Eridu, Mesopotamia. He chose to name his new temple Apsu to signify that all life comes forth from the fresh waters above.

With peace and tranquility now firmly established, Enki began construction on his exalted house. Eridu, the leading city of Sumeria, was ideally situated (north of the Persian Gulf and slightly southwest of Ur) on the Euphrates River. It became known as the city of King Enki, for he had descended from heaven to occupy its throne. Although his father, Enlil, was the original designer of the house, it was Enki who hired human laborers to build its magnificent gardens, its towering ziggurat, and its royal residence. The exterior walls were built with ebony colored sun-baked bricks. Interior walls were overlaid with gold and adorned with a dazzling array of colorful gems. Large quantities of lapis lazuli were used to cover the temple's imposing facade. The same blue stones formed the pavement underneath Enki's throne — which was carved from cedar wood, overlaid with pure gold, and flanked by two majestic eagles with outstretched wings. The fresh water pool placed at the entrance of his temple was stocked with brightly colored carp representing Enki's rulership.

With Inauguration Day, or Akitu (the Babylonian New Year), approaching, Enki would receive the Tablets of the Destinies on which were inscribed words of wisdom and knowledge from his father's oracle. The tablets would become the centerpiece of his reign and the blueprint for governing his kingdom. His royal temple complex now complete, Enki, the god of wisdom, marveled at how it was the perfect representation of his original cosmic temple complete with its three domains: heaven, earth, and the sea.

✡   ✡   ✡

The ANE (Ancient Near East) world is filled with mythological stories of creation that are very similar to the creation account in the Bible. These cosmic myths and legends were likely imitations of the original Biblical record. Cosmos, from the Greek, means universe or a well-ordered system, and the cosmic Temple was the center of the ordered world. G-d's throne, at the center of the universe, was His sacred space. The throne inside the Temple signified the creator, G-d, had triumphed and was enthroned in His sanctuary over the floods that He had subdued (Barker 2010). Exodus (24.10) describes the heavenly throne resting over a "sapphire stone pavement as clear as the sky itself," and the prophet Ezekiel (1.26) reaffirms that it is a "throne that look[s] like sapphire."

> Techelet [blue] is the color of the sea, which resembles the color of the sky, which resembles the color of sapphire, which resembles the color of the Throne of Glory. The Throne of Glory is nothing other than the Temple itself—blue is the very color of the Temple!
>
> (BT *Chullin* 89A)

G-d's kingdom, His Temple, and the cosmos brought stability and an ordered structure which He alone governed. The pattern and construction of His cosmic Temple was designed to preserve the sanctity of His space. Selecting the sacred space was determined by divine oracle. Certain locations held special status as portals through which the gods traversed between heaven and earth. The *rakiah* (firmament), created on the second day, was the portal between these two worlds. This was the Jewish belief in the *Olam Hazeh*, "this world" or the physical world, and the *Olam Haba*, "the world to come" or the world outside of time (represented respectively by earth and heaven). The firmament was the curtain, or veil, placed between the two worlds to keep them separated until creation was restored. It separated the upper male waters from the lower female waters — the waters that, according to tradition, first resisted G-d but were eventually overcome.

In the beginning, that is, before the Creation, the world was but water in water. Then G-d separated the two kinds of water from each other, relegating half of them to the firmament and half of them to the ocean.

(QUOTED IN PATAI 1947: 62)

The earth functioned in much the same way as the firmament; it was the portal between heaven and the sea. The ancients viewed the earth as a flat, disc-shaped platter floating on the waters — heaven above and the seas below. In the ANE, a warrior-god rose up to overcome the seas. The watery abyss was a metaphor for the powers of chaos, the destruction of the ordered world, and ultimately death itself. This motif appears in nearly all the ANE creation stories. Once chaos was defeated, the gods of the ANE built earthly temples on the first dry ground that appeared. Dry ground became the primordial hillock, the platform, or even a mountain upon which a temple was built. G-d's House, for example, was erected on Mount Moriah on the foundation stone (dry ground) which was set over the watery abyss. The sages described this spot as the navel of the world from which all life would come forth. Underneath the altar were shafts that led down to the abyss over which the foundation stone was placed (BT *Sukkah* 49a).

From the Apocalyptic literature of the Second Temple period, watery abyss imagery was quite prevalent. The book of Revelation, for example, describes the cosmic battle that rages at the end of time (which is comparable to G-d's battle against the seas at creation). The seas had come to represent the dominion of the enemy, and ancient literature confirms this thought. In Revelation, we see the Anti-Christ, who is described as a seven-headed beast, coming out of the sea. Not only is he defeated but, in the end, the sea is no more. To defeat the domain of evil, it is necessary to defeat the lower waters. "Then I saw a new heaven and a new earth, for the old heaven and the old earth had passed away and the sea was no longer there" (Rev. 21.1).

Throughout the Bible, G-d's mastery over the seas is a dominant theme. There are numerous examples — from the story of Noah, to the children of Israel crossing the sea, to *Yeshua* walking on water and calming the stormy seas. Once victory was secured, a temple would be built and dedication ceremonies would follow. This is a central theme in the Bible.

The Sea

> The ghosts of the dead tremble beneath the water, with its creatures…He shuts off the view of his throne by spreading his cloud across it. He fixed a circle on the surface of the water, defining the boundary between light and dark. The pillars of heaven tremble, aghast at his rebuke. He stirs up the sea with his power and by his skill he strikes down Rahav. With his Spirit he spreads the heavens; his hand pierces the fleeing serpent.
>
> (JOB 26.5,10-14)

In the beginning, G-d spoke and the cosmos came forth. Darkness hovered over the face of the *tehom* (the deep), and His Spirit hovered over the face of the waters. G-d separated and then restrained the waters of the deep that continually rose up against His rulership. Because this understanding was common among the ancients, the seas aroused a sense of foreboding and fear for the people of the ANE. Mysterious in nature, the seas represented instability and unpredictability — a powerful force capable of destroying everything in its path. Throughout Scripture, the seas are referenced as the domain of beasts and monsters who dwell in the *tehom* and bring destruction upon the earth in the form of catastrophic floods and raging rivers. The seas became the symbol for all that was in rebellion to G-d. Metaphorically, the seas desired to destroy G-d's House, His children, and His Kingdom.

According to scholars, *tehom* was likely the equivalent of

the Babylonian goddess, Tiamat. Just as Tiamat rose up against the gods, the *tehom* confronted G-d for control of the cosmos. Tiamat, in the Babylonian myth tradition, represented chaos and disorder. Tiamat was later identified as Satan. The abyss was another name for the *tehom*.

> O Lord, Almighty G-d of our fathers...who haſt made heaven and earth, with all the ornament thereof; who haſt bound the sea by the word of thy commandment; who haſt shut up the deep, and sealed it by thy terrible and glorious name.
>
> (PRAYER OF MANASSEH 2-3, KJV)

G-d created a boundary marker that the abyss could not pass. This barrier was the firmament which was designed to provide not only stability but a foundation upon which G-d's cosmic House was built. Temples were thought to represent the firmament set in the seas from which the creation arose (Barker 2008: 65).

> Where were you when I laid the foundations of the earth? Tell me, if you have underſtanding. Who determined its measurements? Surely you know! Or who ſtretched the line upon it? To what were its foundations faſtened? Or who laid its cornerſtone... Or who shut in the sea with doors, When it burſt forth and issued from the womb; When I fixed My limit for it, And set bars and doors; When I said, 'This far you may come, but no farther, And here your proud waves muſt ſtop!"
>
> (JOB 38.4-6,8-11 NKJV)

Teeming with great sea monsters, the seas existed outside the boundary of the "courtyards" of heaven and earth. In the same way, wild animals and beasts inhabited the domain outside the wilderness Tabernacle, and they were a threat to anyone who left the safety of the camp. The Bible is filled with this type of imagery. Leviathan, the serpent, the behemoth, and the dragon all have their place in mythology (Ezek. 29.3, Job 40.25). According to the Talmud, the *livyatan* (leviathan) was a giant fish, created on the fifth day of creation, and was the ruler of all the creatures of the sea. The behemoth was a gigantic bull created on the sixth day; like the *livyatan*, he also possessed enormous strength (The Complete Artscroll Siddur 1985: 765). "On that day *Adonai*, with His great, strong, relentless sword, will punish *Livyatan*, the fleeing serpent, the twisting serpent *Livyatan*; He will slay the sea monster" (Is. 27.1).

> G-d has been my king from earliest times, acting to save throughout all the earth. By your strength you split the sea in two, in the water you smashed sea monsters' heads, you crushed the heads of Livyatan and give it as food to the creatures of the desert...
>
> (PS. 74.12-14)

These creatures were synonymous with the four great beasts that came up out of the sea in the book of Daniel (7.2-7). They represented the four gentile empires that oppressed and persecuted Israel throughout her history. In time, the seas came to represent the *goyim* (nations) or the enemies of G-d. In Revelation (13.1), John sees a beast coming out of the sea with ten horns and seven heads. Extra-biblical literature suggests the beast was the ruler of these gentile empires (Rome's Caesar in Revelation).

> You control the raging of the sea; when its waves rear up you calm them. You crushed Rahav like a carcass; with your strong arm you scattered your foes.
>
> (PS. 89:10)

Awake, as in days of old, as in ancient generations! Wasn't it you who hacked Rahav to pieces, you who pierced the sea monster? Wasn't it you who dried up the sea, the waters of the great deep, you who made the sea bottom a road for the redeemed to cross?

(IS. 51.9B-10)

A legend from the Babylonian Talmud explains how King David subdued the subterranean waters before building the Temple. David wanted to build the Lord's Temple on pure, virgin soil — ground that had not yet been disturbed by human hands. However, once he had dug to a depth of fifteen hundred cubits, he came upon a potsherd and concluded someone had already been there. As he dug *shitin* (shafts) underneath the Temple, the Deep arose and threatened to submerge the entire world. It was then that David inscribed the name of G-d on the potsherd and cast it into the Deep so its waves would subside. The Deep obeyed and subsided to a great depth of sixteen thousand cubits.

King David then uttered the fifteen songs (Ps. 120-134), and the Deep re-ascended fifteen thousand cubits (*BT Sukkah 53a,b*). Thus, King David's authority over the Deep was intrinsically linked to the Fifteen Songs of Ascent sung in the Temple — songs which had mythological significance related to primeval events. Scholars connected these songs to various other flood legends and creation myths (Patai 1947). In memory of the creation, these songs eventually became an integral part of the Temple liturgy, including the liturgy of the Water Drawing ceremony at *Sukkot*: a creation renewal ritual.

The Song of the Sea (Ex. 15) recounts Israel's deliverance from Pharaoh and the Egyptian army. In a Torah scroll, the words of the song are structured in a brick-like pattern to resemble the walls of a house. When the sea "split," a wall of water rose on either side; dry ground appeared, just as it did on the third day of creation when the seas were gathered to one place. In creation, the dry ground was the platform/mound that became the foundation for a temple. Israel "walking" on dry ground signified a house built over the waters of chaos. By contrast, Pharaoh, his chariots, and his army drowned in the sea; the waters of the *tehom* closed in around them as they sank like millstones. Based on this event, Pharaoh came to represent the image of a beast in the sea: the great serpent that crouches in the midst of its rivers that G-d will eventually cast into the wilderness (Ezek. 29.3,5).

Temple building and dedication activity followed Israel's triumph over the seas: "This is my G-d and I will build Him a Sanctuary" (Ex. 15.2).

> You shall bring them and implant them on the mount of your heritage, the foundation of your dwelling place which you have made — the sanctuary of your dwelling place that your hands established.
>
> (EX. 15.17)

> G-d was indeed anxious to have a sanctuary erected to Him, it was the condition on which he led them out of Egypt, yea, in a certain sense the existence of all the world depended on the construction of the sanctuary, for when the sanctuary had been erected, the world stood firmly founded.
>
> (L. GINZBERG *Legends of the Jews* VOL. 3: 150)

This pattern is repeated throughout the Bible. At the end of history, when the waters of the abyss are subdued, permanent rest will be established. His House — His creation will be fully restored.

> I saw what looked like a sea of glass mixed with fire. Those defeating the beast, its image and the number of its name were standing by the sea of glass, holding harps which G-d

had given them. They were singing the song of Moses, the servant of G-d, and the song of the Lamb.

(REV. 15.2-3)

From an ANE perspective, the fact that Moses came floating down the Nile River in an ark was a sign of his dominion over the waters of the deep. Pharaoh's daughter, recognizing Moses as a "god" who had defeated the seas, rescued him and raised him to rule over Egypt. When *Yeshua* calmed the raging seas from inside the boat, he was subduing the waters of chaos. The boat was a metaphor for the Temple — a place of safety and stability (Mark 4.35-41). When he walked on the waters over the turbulent seas, he was subduing the abyss and showing himself to be a temple for the living G-d.

> And it came to pass after seven days, that I dreamed a dream by night…there arose a violent wind from the sea, and stirred all its waves. And I beheld, and lo, (the wind caused to come up out of the heart of the seas as it were the form of a man. And I beheld, and lo!) this Man flew with the clouds of heaven…and the voice went out of his mouth, all that heard his voice melted away, as the wax melts when it feels the fire.
>
> (4 EZRA 13.1-4)

In the interpretations for this dream, Messiah is the Man who comes out of the sea. His enemies are the nations of the world, and their final annihilation comes from the fire of the Torah. Perhaps this dream also alludes to *Yeshua* defeating death when he rose from the depths of Sheol: the place of the deep.

The story of Jonah illustrates a similar theme. Jonah was spit out onto dry land after three days and nights in the belly of the fish. Refusing to go to Nineveh, he had boarded a ship for Tarshish — the opposite direction. A violent wind brought on stormy seas that threatened to break the ship apart. The sailors drew lots, and they determined that Jonah was responsible for the calamity. He answered, "I am a Hebrew and I fear *Adonai*, the G-d of heaven, who made both the sea and dry land" (Jonah 1.9). Jonah asked to be thrown overboard to appease the raging seas, and so he was swallowed by the great sea monster, leviathan. In Jonah's prayer for deliverance from the waters of the abyss, he expresses his longing to be in G-d's Temple:

> Out of my distress I called to *Adonai*, and he answered me; from the belly of She'ol, I cried, and you heard my voice. For you threw me into the deep, into the heart of the seas; and the flood enveloped me; all your surging waves passed over me. I thought, 'I have been banished from your sight.' But I will again look at your Holy Temple. The water surrounded me, threatened my life; the deep closed over me, seaweed twined around my head. I was going down to the bottoms of the mountains, to a land whose bars would close me in forever; but you brought me up alive from the pit, *Adonai*, my G-d! As my life was ebbing away, I remembered *Adonai*; and my prayer came in to you into your Holy Temple.
>
> (JONAH 2.3-8)

In the book of Revelation, it is the "land" that comes to the rescue of the sun-clothed woman who has given birth to the male child. She is given the wings of an eagle to fly to her place in the wilderness, and the dragon pursues her in the form of a flood. The woman likely represents the pure, uncontaminated Temple that the first century Qumran community longed for and the reason they settled in the wilderness by the Dead Sea.

> The serpent spewed water like a river out of its mouth after the woman in order to sweep her away in the

flood; but the land came to her rescue — it opened its mouth and swallowed up the river which the dragon had spewed out of its mouth.

(REV. 12.15,16)

The story of Noah and the flood, the main topic in *The Temple Revealed in the Days of Noah, Volume III*, perfectly captures G-d's triumph over His enemies, the seas. As is typical of the pattern, this event is accompanied by temple building and dedication activity. The main purpose of the ark was to preserve the seed and protect future generations from the evil and wickedness of the world. When the fountains of the *tehom* "split," the barrier could no longer restrain the torrents of water that flooded the earth. In time, a Spirit was sent to hover over the earth causing the waters to be subdued and allowing the ark to come to "rest" on a mountain. First century believers likely understood the meaning of this imagery, and they waited for "the day" when *Yeshua* would return, judge the enemies of G-d, and restore creation.

The Temple is often associated with the waters of life, which flow from a spring within the building itself — or rather the Temple is viewed as incorporating within itself such a spring or as having been built upon the spring. The reason that such springs exist in temples is that they were perceived as the primeval waters of creation... The Temple is thus founded upon and stands in contact with the waters of creation. These waters carry the dual symbolism of the chaotic waters that were organized during creation and of the life giving saving nature of the waters of life.

(LUNDQUIST 1984: 57)

Heaven and Earth

The voice of Adonai is over the waters; the G-d of glory thunders, Adonai over rushing waters…the voice of Adonai flashes fiery flames…Adonai sits enthroned above the flood! Adonai sits enthroned as king forever!

(PS. 29.3,7,10)

The first several chapters of the book of Acts take place in Jerusalem's Temple courtyards in the first century CE. This fictional account creates a backstory for the celebration of *Shavuot* (Pentecost) in the Temple precincts and the healing of the crippled man who sat at the Beautiful Gate collecting alms during the festival:

A deep, booming sound reverberated throughout the Temple complex. The *Shacharit* (morning) offerings for *Shavuot* (Pentecost, Feast of Weeks) had concluded, and the unmistakable scent of burnt offerings hung in the air. As the unfamiliar sound intensified, the swelling crowd of worshippers pushed in tightly to fill the Court of the Women. The people watched in sheer amazement as blazing tongues of fire wrapped around the courtyard and then came to rest upon those who followed the Nazarene. The sight of crowd and fire reminded many of a historic day in Israel's history, at the foot of Mount Sinai as they gathered to receive the commandments. On that day, G-d had descended in a fiery smoking furnace atop the mountain — His Holy of Holies — the house of the tongues of fire.

The first commandment, when it left the mouth of the Holy One . . . as meteors and lightening and as torches of fire; a fiery torch to its right and a fiery torch to its left, which burst forth and flew in the air of the heavenly expanse; it proceeded to circle around the camp of Israel.

(TARGUM FRAGMENT TO EX. 20.2 FROM CAIRO GENIZA)

Today the worshippers were awe-struck by this fiery manifestation of the Divine Presence. On the first *Shavuot*, the entire community heard His thundering Voice as they received the Torah of Moses. At Sinai, they saw His Word as a blazing fire coming forth from the Throne of Glory on the mountain. According to Rabbi Yochanan, it was as though G-d spoke each commandment in seventy languages — all of them at once:

> When G-d's voice came forth at Mount Sinai, it divided itself into seventy human languages, so that the whole world might understand it. All at Mount Sinai, young (men) and old, women, children, and infants heard the Voice of G-d according to their ability to understand.
>
> (EXODUS *Rabbah* 5:9)

Those gathered in the Court of Israel prepared for the special offering of *Shavuot*: *Shtei HaLechem*. Two loaves of leavened wheat bread were waved by the *kohanim* (priests) before the altar. From the first of their spring crops, families also brought baskets filled with the seven species of the land (wheat, barley, pomegranates, figs, dates, olives, and grapes). As they handed their offerings to the priests, they took a moment to appreciate the bounty G-d had provided. They recalled their history — how their ancestors had eaten matzah (unleavened bread) at the first Passover in Egypt. They remembered how Israel had been trapped between Pharaoh's army and the sea and how G-d had relegated Pharaoh to the *tehom* (deep). The sea had miraculously split, like a curtain, and G-d's people had walked through on dry ground. They remembered that seven weeks later, at *Shavuot*, Israel had received the *Luchot HaEven* (Tablets of Stone) — formed from the sapphire stone underneath G-d's Throne of Glory.

When the morning ceremonies were over, the worshippers hurried to the homes of family and friends living in

Jerusalem. They caught up on the latest news and enjoyed a fresh meal together before wandering through the backstreets and passageways of the city. There wasn't much time, though — the *Minchah* (afternoon) offerings would soon begin in the Temple.

Peter and John made their way through the crowd and back to the southern steps of the Temple. There they recognized a crippled man whom they had seen on previous occasions. He sat with his hands outstretched — asking for alms. Collecting alms was particularly lucrative at festival time because of the sheer number of pilgrims who came to worship at the Temple. Peter and John confessed that they had no silver or gold to give him; but, they said, they could offer healing in the name of their master, *Yeshua* the Messiah. Peter reached out and pulled the man to his feet. Suddenly, though he had been crippled since birth, the man's ankles strengthened and straightened. He stood on his own power, and he began to walk and leap as he praised G-d. Peter invited him to the Court of the Women — a place that, due to his infirmity, the man had never seen. As he passed through the underground passageway of the Double Gate, the man marveled at the beautifully carved domes in the ceiling. He was mesmerized by the intricate floral and geometric designs and by the vine, leaf, and grape cluster patterns. It was truly an impressive sight. As they approached the court, he gasped at the immense-sized Herodian columns that were part of the stoa (roofed colonnade) — just east of the Court of the Women.

Word of the man's healing reached the Temple leadership who, in response, sent guards to take Peter and John into custody — but not before over five thousand had heard the message and believed in *Yeshua* the Messiah! The following day, the shackled pair were brought before the "godfather" of Jerusalem: the High Priest. Rather than extoll the miraculous healing, the priest demanded to know by what power Peter had healed the crippled man. Peter, filled with the *Ruach* (spirit) — the Wisdom of G-d — spoke eloquently of how *Yeshua,* whom the leadership had executed as a criminal, had risen from the dead and become the true cornerstone of the Temple. It was incomprehensible to these leaders how untrained, unskilled fisherman could possibly speak with such wisdom. They demanded that Peter and John speak no more of *Yeshua* the Messiah, and both men were released to rejoin friends in the city. When their friends heard the report, "they raised their voices to G-d with singleness of heart" (Acts 4.24).

> "Master," they prayed, "you made heaven, earth, the sea and everything in them. By the *Ruach* HaKodesh, through the mouth of our father David, your servant, you said…The kings of the earth took their stand; and the rulers assembled together against *Adonai* and against his Messiah."
>
> (ACTS 4.25A,26)

✡   ✡   ✡

The three cosmic spheres — heaven, earth, and sea — were the pattern for the Temple and the Tabernacle on earth. The seas were represented by the outer courts, the earth by the inner court, and the heavens by the inner chamber: the Holy of Holies. According to Rabbi Pinhas Ben Ya'ir:

> The Tabernacle was made to correspond to the Creation of the world…the heaven, the earth and the sea are houses with bolts. The house of the Holy of Holies was made to correspond to the highest heaven. The outer Holy House was made to correspond to the earth. And the courtyard was made to correspond to the sea…the laver was made to correspond to the sea.
>
> (QUOTED IN PATAI 1947: 108)

Israel's physical journey from Egypt at Passover to the foot of Mount Sinai at *Shavuot* (Feast of Weeks) symbolized their spiritual journey. Egypt, the starting place, signified the underworld (*tehom*) — marked by its pantheon of gods. The seas, which they walked through, represented the outer courts. The wilderness, Israel's temporary home on earth, symbolized the inner courtyards, and the mountaintop at Sinai was the Holy of Holies.

When the redeemed nation finally arrived at the foot of the mountain, it was as though they were prepared to enter the "eternal." The seven-week pilgrimage took them from low levels of spiritual sanctity, in exile in Egypt, to the highest levels, on the mountain, where they became a kingdom of priests.

> When Moses distinguished the Tabernacle into three parts, and allowed two of them to the priests, as a place accessible and common, he denoted the land and the sea, these being of general access to all; but he set apart the third division for G-d, because heaven is inaccessible to men.
>
> (JOSEPHUS *The Antiquities of the Jews* 3.181)

Shavuot comes from the Hebrew sheva meaning seven. A *shavua* is seven days (a week), so *Shavuot* is the plural form for weeks. Temple building and dedication language is always expressed through "sevens" in the Bible (also a common practice in the ANE world). The Sabbath, the seventh, comes from the same root.

> Remember the *Shabbat* to set it apart for G-d. You have six days to labor and do all your work but the seventh is a *Shabbat* for *Adonai* your G-d...For in six days *Adonai* made heaven and earth, the sea and everything in them but on the seventh day he rested. This is why *Adonai* blessed the day, *Shabbat*, and separated it for himself.
>
> (EX. 20.8-10A,11)

Rest signified a temple built, filled with all the appropriate vessels and furniture, and ready for the services to be performed. Rest also indicated the raging waters of chaos had been subdued and all of G-d's enemies destroyed. The purpose and function of the House could now be fully realized, that is, to be fruitful, multiply, and fill the earth.

> The Temple and its furnishings did possess cosmic symbolism. Such features were designed to stress the divine power over the created order and to establish the Temple as a source of blessing for the land and people of Israel. The underlying idea was that the Temple was a microcosm of the macrocosm so that the building gave visual expression to the belief in Yahweh's dominion over the world... thus the Temple building signified the cosmic rule of G-d who was worshipped there.
>
> (R.E. CLEMENTS 1965: 67)

Peter and John's story in Acts (3.1-4.26) refers to a prayer in the Temple liturgy that states G-d made heaven, earth, the sea, and everything that "filled" those three realms (Ps.146.6). The psalmist describes G-d's acts of power: justice for the oppressed, freedom for the prisoners, sight for the blind, and the lifting of those bent low. "At the Zenith of the universe is your dwelling, and your justice and righteousness extend to the ends of the earth" (from the Shema blessings). The worshippers who had gathered in the Temple that day undoubtedly understood G-d's mastery over the cosmos and over the worthless gods of this world.

> You are *Adonai*, you alone. You made heaven, the heaven of heavens, with all their array, the earth and all the things that are in it, the seas and all that is in them; and you preserve them all. The army of heaven worships you.
>
> (NEH. 9.6)

A similar story is told (Acts 14) of a man crippled from birth, living in Lystra, who responded to the Good News of the Kingdom. Upon hearing the Word shared by the Apostle Paul, the man jumped up and began to walk. The stunned crowd compared Paul and Barnabus to their own gods, Zeus and Hermes, and they proceeded to bring offerings in their honor. Paul admonished the crowd to turn from those worthless things and to serve the "living G-d who made heaven, earth, the sea and everything in them."

The book of Revelation refers to the Exodus (20.11) passage, emphasizing that G-d alone has dominion over all three realms of the cosmos: heaven, earth, and the sea. In His cosmic Temple, the world outside of time, all His enemies are destroyed. His house and His throne are established, and He has filled His house with all good things: justice, righteousness, mercy, and truth.

> Then the angel I saw standing on the sea and on the land
> lifted his right hand toward heaven and swore by the One
> who lives forever and ever, who created heaven and what is
> in it, earth and what is in it, and the sea and what is in it.
>
> (REV. 10.5,6A)

The Firmament

> *Halleluyah! Praise G-d in his holy place! Praise him in the*
> *heavenly dome of his power! Praise him for his mighty deeds!*
> *Praise him for his surpassing greatness!*
>
> (PS. 150.1,2)

On the second day of creation, G-d placed a *rakiah* (firmament) in the heavens to separate the waters above from the waters below. Separation is the Hebrew concept of *kedushah* or holiness (see chapter 3): to be set apart with restrictions applied. *Kedushah* is also a term for the creation process whereby two things (male and female) are set apart for a specific function and purpose: to produce new life.

The Ramban (Nachmanides, born in Spain in 1194 CE) suggested the *rakiah* was one of the great mysteries of creation. He explained it as a spiritual separation between two worlds: the physical (this world) and the eternal (the world to come). Philo referred to the firmament as the boundary between the visible and invisible creations. The *rakiah*, which means to hammer, to flatten out, or to spread out, was the vast expanse over the earth reflecting blue from the waters above. "You have donned glory and majesty covering with light as with a garment stretching out the heavens like a curtain" (Ps. 104:2 Artscroll Siddur).

The curtain in front of the Holy of Holies represented the firmament — the place where two worlds become one. Behind the veil, the Holy of Holies symbolized the eternal world.

As the firmament had been created on the second day to divide the waters, which were under the firmament from the waters which were above, so there was a curtain in the Tabernacle to divide between the holy and the most holy.

(L. GINZBERG *Legends of the Jews* VOL. 3:150)

The firmament was created to provide stability and order to the universe — also the primary function of a temple. "The Temple, the place of G-d's throne, stood in the midst of the seas and represented the firmament which the creator had established and continued to maintain for his people" (Barker 2008: 67). The *rakiah* was thought to preserve the created order and to protect the world from the *tehom* (deep) or the abyss.

I made the shore the limit for the sea; by eternal decree it cannot pass. Its waves may toss, but to no avail; although they roar, they cannot cross it.

(JER. 5.22B)

Early Christian writers saw the Tabernacle's partitions as the division of the universe with its upper and lower world and a firmament in between:

> Since therefore it had been shown him how G-d made the heaven and the earth and how on the second day he made the firmament in the middle between them and thus made the one place into two places so Moses in like manner in accordance with the pattern which he had seen made the Tabernacle into two — an inner and outer.
>
> (COSMAS INDICOPLEUTUS Christian Topography 2.35)

Jerusalem was the point where the eternal world and the natural world converged. On earth as it is in heaven meant that the earthly temple, with its services and ceremonies, was modeled after the heavenly one. The priests serving in the Temple on earth were counterparts to the angels serving in the Temple above. This is an important key for unlocking the book of Revelation and for understanding much of what *Yeshua* taught about the Kingdom.

The prophet Ezekiel received a vision of the creation Temple from the viewpoint of the Holy of Holies. His prophetic message was given to provide hope to those in exile in Babylon: the House of G-d would be restored. Ezekiel mourned the loss of the Divine Presence from the First Temple as he also mourned the loss of his own precious wife. He saw G-d's Temple as a bride and a wife — a common understanding in the ancient world. Some of the language in the book of Ezekiel is highly cryptic and very difficult to understand. Chapter one, for example, alludes to the *Ma'aseh*

Merkavah, the "works of the chariot." This is a unique glimpse into the eternal world of the Holy of Holies with its chariot throne atop the sapphire stone pavement:

> Above the *rakiah*...was the appearance of sapphire stone in the likeness of a throne and upon the likeness of the throne was a likeness like the appearance of a man upon it, from above. And I saw the color of chashmal (type of angel), like the appearance of fire inside it all around...I saw something like the appearance of fire and a brilliance surrounding it.
>
> (EZEK. 1.26-27 ARTSCROLL STONE ED.)

> Moses departed from the heavens with the two tables on which ten-commandments were engraved and they were made of sapphire-like stone.
>
> (L. GINZBERG *Legends of the Jews* VOL. 3:118)

> The sapphire, used for the tables, was taken from the Throne of Glory.
>
> (VOL. 6:49)

Only the high priest could pass beyond the veil to enter the Holy of Holies, and this could only be done on one day each year: Yom Kippur (Day of Atonement). The veil (Ex. 26.33) which separated the Holy Place from the Holy of Holies was woven in the same colors as the high priest's garments: blue, scarlet, purple, and linen (2 Chr. 3.14). Clement of Alexandria suggested "purple is from water, linen from the earth; blue, being dark, is like the air, as scarlet is like fire."

Now the vestment of the high priest being made of linen signified the earth; the blue denoted the sky...he also appointed the breastplate to be placed in the middle of the ephod, to resemble the earth, for that has the very middle place of the world. And the girdle, which encompassed the high priest round, signified the ocean for that goes round about and includes the universe.

(JOSEPHUS The Antiquities of the Jews 3.184-185)

Sirach refers to the Temple as the House of the veil (50.5,11). According to Josephus, the veil, which represented the cosmos, was ornately embroidered with a panoramic picture of the heavens:

But before these doors, there was a veil of equal largeness with the doors. It was a Babylonian curtain, embroidered with blue, and fine linen, and scarlet and purple, and of a contexture that was truly wonderful. Nor was this mixture of colors without its mystical interpretation, but was a kind of image of the universe; for by the scarlet there seemed to be enigmatically signified fire, by the fine flax the earth, by the blue the air, and by the purple the sea; two of them having their colors the foundation of this resemblance... This curtain had also embroidered upon it all that was mystical in the heavens, excepting that of the [twelve] signs, representing living creatures.

(JOSEPHUS The Wars of the Jews 5.212-213)

...but then they spread over the Tabernacle veils of fine linen and purple, and blue, and scarlet colors embroidered... This veil was very ornamental, and embroidered with all sorts of flowers which the earth produces; and there were interwoven into it all sorts of variety that might be an ornament, excepting the forms of animals.

(JOSEPHUS The Antiquities of the Jews 3.124,126)

The book of Revelation reveals a graphic picture of the defiled Second Temple which is personified by the great harlot sitting upon the beast and dressed in purple and scarlet. The beast with seven heads and ten horns represented foreign rulers who controlled many administrative functions in the Temple. This "alliance" caused the Temple and the priesthood to become impure and corrupt; as a result, the Temple and the city of Jerusalem were destroyed by Rome in 70 CE. This symbolism was eventually applied to the city of Rome itself:

> Come, I will show you the judgment of the great whore who is sitting on many waters. He carried me off in the Spirit to a desert, and I saw a woman sitting on the scarlet beast filled with blasphemous names and having seven heads and ten horns. The woman was dressed in purple and scarlet and glittered with gold, precious stones and pearls.
>
> (REV. 17.1B,3)

The Hebrew Book of Enoch (3 Enoch is a fifth century CE text attributed to Rabbi Ishmael who died before the Bar Kokhba revolt in 132 CE) explains how the veil divides this world from the world beyond time. The writer saw a vision from the perspective of the Holy of Holies looking back through the veil towards the earth. The veil, he said, provides a view of the future from the perspective of eternity; it represents all history seen simultaneously. R. Ishmael saw the course of human history, from Adam to the Messianic age, embroidered on the curtain. "Come and I will show you the curtain…which is spread before the Holy One on which are printed all the generations of the world and all their deeds"(45.1). Daniel, Ezekiel, Zechariah, Moses, and John were each given similar visions from inside the Holy of Holies: the world outside of time.

The veil conceals the mysteries of the deity where only the Prince of the Divine Presence is allowed to go. *Yeshua*, in passing through the veil of the Temple, was moving beyond the firmament barrier to permanently enter the Holy of Holies in heaven:

At that moment the parokhet (veil) in the Temple was ripped in two from top to bottom; and there was an earthquake with rocks splitting apart.

(MATT. 27.51)

He departed "this world," and he entered the "world to come" in order to sit at the right hand of G-d as the Prince of the Presence and the High Priest of heaven. Understanding the nature of the two worlds reduces some of the confusion surrounding the book of Hebrews. The greater covenant is the "Creation Covenant" restored — over which *Yeshua* the Messiah serves as mediator. He is the High Priest of the cosmic Temple who makes intercession on our behalf.

Therefore, since we have a great Cohen Gadol [High Priest] who has passed through to the highest heaven, *Yeshua* the Son of G-d, let us hold firmly to what we acknowledge as true. Therefore, let us confidently approach the throne from which G-d gives grace, so that we may receive mercy and find grace in our time of need.

(HEB. 4.14,16)

The veil is split, and the way is open, but we cannot physically enter that realm. It is the role of the Holy Spirit to pass through the portal between heaven and earth and to give us access to the throne. This is only possible, however, when we confess, repent, and turn from our sin.

Overcoming the flood

For at His Word the storm-wind arose, lifting up towering waves. The sailors were raised up to the sky then plunged into the depths. In their trouble they cried to Adonai, and he rescued them from their distress. He silenced the storm and stilled its waves, and they rejoiced, as the sea grew calm.

Then he brought them safely to their destined port.

What do we do when the enemy comes in like a flood? Life's storms are raging with ever-increasing intensity. We are threatened with wave after wave of distress and uncertainty. The world is filled with untold heartbreak and sorrow. The works of the flesh continue to destroy the very fabric of society. Some have left their first love to run after the gods of this world. It often feels like the enemy is in total control while the people of G-d are in retreat. Many fear that G-d has removed His protective hedge and now the full fury of the treacherous waters has been unleashed. Some are drowning in anxiety, worry, doubt, and fear — exhausted from fighting battles that overwhelm even the strongest families. Others have simply lost hope.

In order to rebuild the house, the enemy must first be defeated. The real battle takes place in the mind, and that is where our fight must begin. This requires that we "take every thought captive and make it obey the messiah" (2 Co. 10.4). Paul reminds us not to be conformed to the thinking of this world but to be transformed daily by the renewing of our minds (Rom. 12.2). The mind is the battlefield where our greatest successes, as well as our greatest failures, take place.

Being "filled" with the Word of G-d is the key to victory — not in a cursory or superficial way but as a systematic and daily discipline. Some do not understand, or simply have never experienced, the supernatural power of the Word of G-d: the power to heal, to transform, to rescue, and to deliver. Exercising discernment and reinforcing our mental gates must become part of our daily training. Everything must be judged before it is allowed entrance into the "house."

For the word of G-d is living and powerful, and sharper

than any two-edged sword, piercing even to the division of soul and spirit, and of joints and marrow, and is a discerner of the thoughts and intents of the heart.

(HEB. 4.12 NKJB)

The psalms are an excellent place to focus daily, intensive study. They represent the deepest expressions of the human heart and cover the full gamut of emotion. They communicate the heartfelt longing of the soul for G-d, and they remind us of His love and concern for the brokenhearted and those crushed in spirit. As the hymnal for the Second Temple, the Psalms played a vital role in the services, ceremonies, and offerings.

The fifteen Songs of Ascent (Ps. 120-134) are a great place to begin. These psalms are unique in that they present a pattern for mankind's journey on earth—a journey that begins in exile, separated from G-d, and ends at the mountain in His Presence. The number fifteen, according to the sages, represents the highest level of worship to G-d. Fifteen is the value of His Name, Yah. The Temple worship structure is built around the number fifteen. There are fifteen steps of a Passover seder, and there were fifteen steps before the Nicanor Gate where the Levitical choir sung. "On the fifteen steps which led into the women's court, corresponding with fifteen songs of degrees, stood the Levites with their musical instruments and sang" (Mishnah *Sukkah* 5.4-5). The Aaronic benediction (The Lord bless you and keep you...) is composed of fifteen words, and there were fifteen superintendents that oversaw the daily operation of the Temple. The fifteen Songs of Ascent were sung as the worshippers made their way to Jerusalem for the three pilgrimage festivals: *Pesach* (Passover), *Shavuot* (Feast of Weeks/Pentecost) and *Sukkot* (Feast of Tabernacles). It has been suggested that these psalms were also sung by the returning exiles from Babylon as they made their final ascent to Jerusalem. Our spiritual journey is intended to take us ever closer to the Presence of G-d. But if we don't take hold of our thought life, if we fail to rewire our thinking, we may well find ourselves in exile and cast from His Presence.

Psalm 121 begins, "I raise my eyes to the mountains, where does my help come from? My help comes from the Lord, maker of heaven and earth." The psalmist reminds us of G-d's promises to continuously guard and protect our souls and forever keep us from every evil. Psalm 122 speaks of the unity of the tribes of Israel in the city of unity — Jerusalem — the place where the thrones of the House of David will be set up. Psalm 125 reminds us that, "As the mountains surround Jerusalem, the Lord surrounds his people now and forevermore." Psalm 127 declares that "Unless the Lord builds the house, the workers build in vain." These Songs of Ascent, which were part of the Temple liturgy, were ultimately linked to the restoration of all creation.

We are one body with many members who are all interconnected (1 Co. 12.12). Each member has a specific function and purpose in building the House. Knowing your purpose and calling is a great gift, and by embracing your call you will stand in the center of His will: the safest and most secure place on earth. When the floods come and the torrents beat against the House, it cannot be shaken because it is well constructed. It is built upon a firm foundation with *Yeshua* as our chief cornerstone.

If *Adonai* hadn't been for us when people rose to attack us,
then, when their anger blazed against us,
they would have swallowed us alive!
Then the water would have engulfed us,
The torrent would have swept over us.
Yes, the raging water would have swept over us.
Blessed be *Adonai* who did not leave us
to be a prey for their teeth!
We escaped like a bird from the hunter's trap;
the trap is broken and we have escaped.
Our help is in the Name of *Adonai*,
The maker of heaven and earth.

(PS. 124.2-8)

CHAPTER THREE

SEPARATION AND UNITY

In the beginning when G-d made the heaven and earth as one house…he divided into two portions that fabric of the universe although it was but one house…that the upper portion might afford a dwelling place to angels and the lower to men.
(Clementine Recognitions 1.27)

Beresheet, "In the beginning," reveals the unity of G-d's sacred space. This unity is expressed as One Day or Yom Echad (Gen. 2.5 And there was evening and there was morning One Day). In the creation week, G-d began to separate His cosmic Temple into two parts: this world (darkness) and the world to come (light). The subsequent days of creation, each separated from the first day, were given a particular function in the construction of the cosmic Temple. When the house was complete, the separated days re-joined to again become a *Yom Echad* (One Day) — now called the seventh day: the Sabbath.

According to John Walton, the creation week was not a list of material substances but rather a depiction of how G-d's cosmic Temple should function. Walton proposed that *time* was the function of day one (the separation between this world and the world to come), *weather* was the function of day two, *food production* was the function of day three, *agriculture* was the function of day four (based on the role of functionaries: the great luminaries), fish teeming in the sea and birds flying in the air were the functions of day five, and the creation of mankind to reproduce and fill the earth was the function of day six (Walton 2009: 53-58). Mankind's role was, therefore, to populate the world without limitation and to serve as priests over G-d's creation. This allowed for the proper functioning of G-d's cosmic Temple. "In the ancient world something came into existence when it was separated out as a distinct entity, given a function and given a name" (Walton 2006: 180).

The seventh day, a return to *Yom Echad*, represented the unity of the previous six days and signified that the Temple was finished and ready to be dedicated. This is the backdrop for John's throne room vision in Revelation (chapters 4,5) as well as Zechariah's vision in chapter fourteen:

> It will be on That Day the light will not be either very bright or very dim. It will be a *Yom Echad*; it will be known as *HaShem's*, neither day nor night, but it will happen towards evening time that there will be light.
>
> (ZECH. 14.6,7 ARTSCROLL STONE ED.)

Creation was a gradual process of separation and unity. Female elements were separated from male: earth from heaven, waters below from waters above, night from day, darkness from light, dry land from gathered seas, six days from seven, and Eve from Adam. Woman was separated from man in order to "create" a relationship in which two would become one, produce life, and establish a house for future generations. "The one created in the image of the Holy One is created male and female — and then separated into two — because both are required to make creation into a dwelling place for the Creator" (Patterson 2005: 22).

> If the female had not been separated from the male, she would not die with the male. His separation was the origin of death. For this Christ came so that he might correct the separation that existed from the beginning by uniting two together.
>
> (GOSPEL OF PHILIP 70)

"And thus were completed (kallah) the heaven and the earth and all their hosts. G-d completed (kallah) on the seventh day His work which He had made" (Gen. 2.1,2). The Hebrew word kallah can also be translated "bride." The sages saw heaven and earth, G-d's cosmic Temple, adorned as a beautiful bride on the seventh day. In Jewish liturgy, the Shabbat (seventh) is compared to a bride and is called G-d's Shekinah or indwelling presence.

Adam could not bear children himself, and so it was not good for man to be alone. G-d separated from Adam "one who helps": an ahzar. From the word ahzar we get azarah: the inner courtyard of the temple. Just as Eve was created to help Adam and to bring fruitfulness to their house, so too the services performed in the inner courtyard were designed to help Israel draw near to G-d and to bring blessing and fruitfulness to the nation.

> The first of the Inner Courtyards was known as the Court of the Women (Ezrat Nashim). Fifteen steps led up to the most important and highest level courtyard known as the Azarah. Within this courtyard were two

sub-courtyards, the Court of Israel (*Ezrat Yisrael*) and the Court of the Priests (*Ezrat Kohanim*).

(JOSEPH GOOD A Day in the Temple)

By the G-d of your father, who will help (*ahzar*) you, by *El Shaddai*, who will bless you with blessings from heaven above, blessings from the deep lying below, blessings from breasts and the womb.

(GEN. 49.25)

Clay Trumball, in his book *The Threshold Covenant*, describes ancient Polynesian myth stories in which the children of Mother Earth and Father Sky forced their parents apart so the world could exist between them. He explained that various cosmogonies characterize creation as a process marked by stages of separation. This is key: Creation is the process of "cutting" between the upper world (male) and the lower world (female) "to form a distinction crucial to the *relation* that defines creation" (Patterson 2005: 156). *Brit*, which means "cut," is the Hebrew word for covenant. In the ancient world, cutting into two parts was necessary for the confirmation of a covenantal relationship. In light of this, it is important to note that the earth was "cut" from heaven just as Eve was "cut" from Adam so they could come together and produce life.

The unity between heaven and earth on the seventh day represented the completion of G-d's house: "the generations (*toldot*) of the heaven and earth when they were created" (Gen. 2.4). *Toldot* means "to bear children" suggesting heaven and earth became a cosmic house, metaphorically speaking, for producing offspring. The expression, "when they were created" (*b'hee'bar'am*) can be re-arranged to spell "through *Avraham*." This is noteworthy because it was *Avraham* who obeyed the call of G-d by *separating* himself from the idolatry of his day and crossing over to possess the land. It was only after this separation that Sarah, who had been barren outside the land, produced the promised seed, Isaac.

Kedushah (holiness), the term for separation, comes from the root *kadosh* which means "to be set apart or to differentiate." To be *set apart* implies certain restrictions. "The *kedushah* of periods of *time* such as the Sabbath and the festivals is marked by limits on man's activities of work and construction" (Berman 1995: 6). In the Temple environment, elements were set apart for the service of G-d by formal, legal restrictions and limitations. These restrictions protected the sanctity of the sacred space in which the priests, the Levites, and the men of Israel performed their various duties. In particular, ceremonies related to the laws of ritual purity preserved the separation between life inside the Temple and death outside. All the laws of purity dealt with raising one's spiritual status after a death of some kind.

In the garden, the Tree of the Knowledge of Good and Evil was also set apart with certain restrictions; Adam and Eve were forbidden to eat its fruit. *The Hymns of Paradise*, written by Ephrem in the fourth century CE, compare Paradise to a mountain whose summit is the Holy of Holies. One Hymn likens the Tree of Knowledge to the veil in the Temple — separating this world from the world to come:

> In the very midst he planted the Tree of Knowledge, endowing it with awe, hedging it with dread, so that it might straightway serve as a boundary to the inner region of Paradise. In the midst of Paradise, G-d had planted the Tree of Knowledge to separate off, above and below, sanctuary from Holy of Holies.
>
> (3.3,14)

Adam and Eve ate from the forbidden tree. Their rebellion led not only to their own death but also to the disintegration of creation itself. Violating the rules of His house had serious consequences. To prevent sin's deadly effects from contaminating the sacred space, it had to be removed. The Creation Covenant had been breached, and exile was the judgment. Death separated Adam and Eve from the garden sanctuary and from His Divine Presence, and a barrier was erected to prevent them from entering back.

Slowly, Adam and Eve's physical bodies began to decay and the cosmos began to disintegrate. Creation was in need of restoration...."because the creation itself also will be delivered from the bondage of corruption into the glorious liberty of the children of G-d." We know "the whole creation groans and labors with birth pangs together until now" (Rom. 8.21,22 NKJV). Here Paul describes the restoration of creation in the language of physical reproduction (as in the *toldot* of heaven and earth). Paul goes on to say that creation's renewal began with the resurrection of Messiah *Yeshua* who makes intercession on our behalf and establishes unity with G-d.

> For I am convinced that neither death nor life, neither angels nor other heavenly rulers, neither what exists or what is coming, neither powers above nor powers below, nor any other created thing will be able to separate us from the love of G-d which comes to us through the Messiah *Yeshua*, our Lord.
>
> (ROM. 8.38,39)

To Be Holy

Our modern view of holiness (*kedushah*) is slightly skewed. We generally ascribe holiness to an individual's behavior: to those who act righteously or with piety or exercise the right moral conduct. Holiness, however, has more to do with function and making distinctions between elements than it does with character quality. Holiness is ascribed to G-d and the functions of His

House: the high priest sprinkled the blood in the Holy of Holies and on the holy curtain, the priests stood on holy ground, Israel worshipped at His holy mountain, the high priest was anointed with holy oil, the priests wore holy garments and performed services during holy convocations, the people spoke in the holy tongue, and they rested on the Sabbath — the first entity to be declared holy in the Bible. "G-d blessed the seventh day and sanctified (*kadosh*) it, because on it He rested from all His work which G-d had created and made" (Gen. 2.2). Collectively, the Body of Messiah is His Spiritual Temple and His "holy ones."

Holiness/separation is invariably connected to the Temple and its services. The garden sanctuary on the mountain of G-d featured a threshing floor where life-giving grain seed was "separated" from worthless chaff. In fact, the Hebrew word "to thresh," *daish*, means "to separate." This may explain why David purchased the threshing floor located atop Mount Moriah in Jerusalem as *the* place to build a House for G-d. At the threshing floor, Adam was separated from the dust of the earth to become the first man. At the threshing floor, the land of Israel was separated from all other lands. The children of Israel were separated from the nations, the men of Israel were separated from the people, the Levites were separated from the men of Israel, the priests were separated from the Levites, and the high priest was separated from the priests. Each group had their own specific role and function in preserving the seed of life and in bringing fruitfulness to the whole world: the purpose for *kedushah*.

The temple was *the* place that separated the physical world, pictured in the six days of creation, from the eternal, seventh day. Philo explains the significance of the number six:

> And he says that the world was made in six days, not because the Creator stood in need of a length of time... but because the things created required arrangement; and number is akin to arrangement; and, of all numbers, six is, by the laws of nature, the most productive: for of all

the numbers...it is the first perfect one, being made equal to its parts, and being made complete by them...and, so to say, it is formed so as to be both male and female, and is made up of the power of both natures...It was fitting therefore, that the world, being the most perfect of created things, should be made according to the perfect number, namely, six...since it was to embrace the character both of the male who sows the seed, and of the female who receives it. And he allotted each of the six days to one of the portions of the whole, taking out the first day, which he does not even call the first day, that it may not be numbered with the others, but entitling it one, he names it rightly, perceiving in it, and ascribing to it the nature and appellation of the limit.

(PHILO *On the Creation*, III 13-15)

The sixth day, *Yom Ha-Shishi*, is the only day in the creation week that begins with the definite article "the," the Hebrew letter *hey*. This letter, when added to *Avram's* name, forms *Avraham*. Rabbi Culi, in his work *Me'am Lo'ez*, suggested that the firmament created on the second day to form the separation between the upper and lower waters was a foreshadowing of *Avraham* who was born during the second millennium. He believed that *Avraham* was the first human to form a separation between those who believed in the One True G-d and those who did not.

"When they were created" (*b'hee'bar'am*) contains a diminished letter *hey*. So, the sages proposed, *Avraham* would become the father of many nations and a pillar in the House of Israel in the physical realm. The sages long believed that G-d created heaven and earth for the sake of *Avraham* and that his faith would ultimately sustain the world. It all began when *Avraham* separated himself and his family from his father's world of idols to claim as his inheritance the land of Canaan: the future location of the Holy Temple.

✡   ✡   ✡

Very little is known about the enigmatic figure Nimrod or the circumstances surrounding *Avraham's* journey to the land of Israel. This vignette invents a relationship between the two and assumes the opinion of some scholars who suggest *Avraham* resided in the Hurrian region of northern Mesopotamia instead of farther south in Sumer:

Nimrod feared an heir from the line of Shem would rise up and take control of *his* kingdom. In an effort to increase his power and preserve his empire, Nimrod forced many of Shem's descendants to migrate west and north from central Mesopotamia. He was convinced that if he first consolidated the city-states of Akkad, and then assumed the role of national god and imperial monarch, the threat posed by Shem's line would disappear. Nimrod was often referred to as *the continuing seed of rebellion* because he manipulated his descendants, through trickery and deceit, into rebelling against the One True G-d. Rumors spread that his grandfather, Ham, had stolen the high priestly coats of skin that were originally Adam's and had given them to Nimrod. Nimrod wore the skins, for in his mind they provided a stamp of approval on his god-like rulership.

In response to Nimrod's oppressive tactics, Terah moved north to the land of the Hurrians where the Tigris and Euphrates cross the upper reaches of the Fertile Crescent. This region featured rugged mountains and high plains, and it was an important crossroads for international trade and commerce. The Hurrians imported obsidian from Anatolia, high quality lapis lazuli from the Indus Valley, and the ever-prized cedar wood from Lebanon. The region's capital, Ur-Kesh (some scholars think extra letters were added to Ur-Kesh to form Ur Kasdim /Chaldees/), was an affluent, cosmopolitan city whose buildings boasted intricately detailed architecture, ornate stonework, and even indoor plumbing. Vibrant marketplaces teemed with luxury items such as expensive jewelry and unusual musical instruments. Rows of empty cattle carts and donkey caravans parked along the narrow, tree-lined streets sat waiting for tradesmen and merchants to load them with costly wares.

At one point, *Avram's* father, Terah, served as governor of this bustling metropolis. Terah married Amthelo, daughter of the King of Ur-Kesh, and enjoyed the riches, power, and influence that came with his position in society. His gubernatorial status afforded him an opulent lifestyle complete with palatial accommodations encircled by luxuriant gardens. The grounds of his estate featured twelve large stone statues finely chiseled by Hurrian craftsmen. Towering walls of shrubbery-draped stone surrounded the property that Terah shared with his wife and their three sons: *Avram,* Nahor, and Haran. The youngest son, Haran, was born and raised in Ur-Kesh in these lavish surroundings. After Haran's early death, *Avram* married Haran's daughter, Sarai, and also assumed responsibility for raising his son, Lot.

In time, Terah lost his appointment in Ur-Kesh forcing the family to return to the city of Charan: the birthplace of *Avram* and Nahor. Located a hundred miles to the west of Ur-Kesh, Charan was built on an enormous crest that provided natural fortifications for the city. Springs flowed up from its base, and a ziggurat (the mirror image of one constructed in Ur in Sumer) was erected nearby. Charan's chief god, like in Ur, was Nanna the god of the moon. Located along a popular trade route, Charan was politically stable and economically flourishing. Terah was more than happy to live out his final days there, although he could not shake the profound sadness he felt as *Avram* loaded his family and possessions and departed in a caravansary for the land of his ancestor, Shem. Terah, brushing aside a tear as he watched the family set off, reflected back on the miracle of *Avram's* birth.

On a calm night, seventy-five years earlier, Nimrod and his stargazers witnessed an exploding star in the east. The light from the star blanketed the entire night sky, and Nimrod's astrologers interpreted the celestial omen as a *sign* that Terah's newborn son, *Avram*, would kill Nimrod and ascend the throne. Terrified, Nimrod demanded *Avram* be put to death. Terah's wife, Amthelo, stole away under the cover of darkness — making her way east to hide in the vast network of caves in the Zagros Mountains. As tears rolled down her swollen, red face, she clung tightly to *Avram* and prayed fervently to the One True G-d — asking Him to spare her first-born son.

Amthelo settled in a large, underground chamber completely mesmerized by the crystal-lined walls that never stopped their glittering. Amthelo sent word to Shem, *Avram's* forefather, to come and instruct him in the ways of the One True G-d: creator of the sun, moon, and stars and ruler over the heavens, earth, and seas. She had heard many inspiring stories throughout her lifetime, and she knew that Shem was the rightful heir and high priest of the family. She had heard rumors of a book that contained the celestial secrets of creation, and she anxiously waited for Shem to pass the book of mysteries along to the one who was ten generations from Noah: her son, *Avram*. Shem sat with *Avram* and explained in rich detail the creation, the garden sanctuary, and the ways of the high priest. He expounded on the forms of history, the destiny of the generations of his family, and the mysteries behind the heavenly curtain that separated G-d from the world. Noah, Shem's father, had carefully preserved the treasured book inside a specially constructed golden chest that he built before the floodwaters rose. After Noah offered his burnt offering atop the mountain called Moriah, he presented the book to Shem. It is believed that King Solomon was given the wisdom contained in this book of mysteries so he could construct the first temple to the One True G-d on that very same spot.

When *Avram* reached his thirteenth birthday, it was safe to return to Ur-Kesh. Akkad had been conquered, Nimrod's power in the region had been greatly diminished, and his father, Terah, was now governor. While Terah was achieving great financial and social success in Hurrian society, *Avram* was learning the ways of a shepherd — guarding and caring for his flocks and herds in the mountainous terrain of the Zagros. After losing the governorship, Terah's entire family returned to Charan. For fourteen more years, *Avram* waited patiently — shepherding his flocks at the edge of the Fertile Crescent until one dark, moonless night when the Lord G-d spoke to him:

> *Lech Lecha* (Go for) yourself from your land, from your relatives, and from your father's house to the land that I will show you. And I will make of you a great nation; I will bless you and make your name great and you shall be a blessing. I will bless those who bless you, and to him who curses you I will curse; and all the families of the earth shall bless themselves by you.
>
> (GEN. 12.1-3 ARTSCROLL STONE ED.)

Although *Avram's* decision to leave Charan meant separating from family relationships and the comforts of Hurrian society, the only thing that mattered to him was moving west towards the ancient site of the garden sanctuary and the dwelling place of His G-d. This was the most honorable path. So *Avram* packed his entire household, along with his nephew Lot, and headed south through Tadmor to Damascus. From there, the family traveled around the southern edge of the snow-capped peaks of Mount Hermon — heading west to cross the Upper Jordan's surging river. At Dan, they finally stepped foot upon the land of promise — entering through a massive triple-arched gate built of sun-dried mud bricks. Once in the land, they journeyed on: first to Hazor, then south to Meggido, and finally to Shechem where they ended their long trek. Shechem's terrain was somewhat steep and rocky — perfect for shepherding *Avram's* flocks.

Two Became One

The biblical world view is a vision of the unity of all things and how the visible material world relates to another dimension of existence that unites all things into one divinely ordained system known as the eternal covenant, the Creation Covenant.

(BARKER 2010: 19)

After *Avram* separated from his earthly father in Mesopotamia, he crossed over into Canaan to join in covenant with his heavenly Father and to take possession of the land. Their union meant *Avram* would bear much fruit. Therefore, after the letter *hey* was added to his name, *Avraham* became the "father of many nations." According to the sages, G-d created the world with the letter *hey* to symbolize the birth of the Messianic Kingdom — where seed sown would produce a great harvest. Rabbi *Gamliel* said, "In the Messianic era women will bear children every day like a hen which lays eggs every day" (Quoted in Patai 1979: 230). *Avraham* and Sarah (formerly *Avram* and *Sarai*) were given a promise that together they would produce fruit in such abundance that their offspring would be as many as the stars in the heavens and the grains of sand on the seashore. This was the Good News.

> And then shall the whole earth be tilled in righteousness,
> And shall all be planted with trees and be full of blessing...
> And as for all seed which is sown thereon,
> Each measure shall bear a thousand,
> And each measure of olives shall yield ten presses of oil.
>
> (1 ENOCH 10.18,19)

Avraham's first possession in the land of Israel was the Cave of Macpelah which he purchased as a burial plot for his wife, Sarah. Macpelah means "double" and represents the bond between husband and wife. This cave, a metaphor for the inner chamber of the temple, was the place where the patriarchs and matriarchs — including Adam and Eve — were buried. The sages theorized that the Cave of Macpelah was the entrance to the Garden of Eden beneath the throne of Glory: the place where heaven and earth unite as one.

The function and purpose of creation was to fashion order out of non-order: to produce new life and to build relationships. Male and female elements were first separated then re-united to build a house that perfectly reflected the image of G-d. This is *the* theme of the Bible. *Yeshua* told the Pharisees that in the beginning G-d created Adam and Eve male and female. He said that a man should separate from his father and mother and unite with his wife so that the two would become one flesh. "Thus they are no longer two but one. So then no one should split apart what G-d has joined together" (Matt 19.4-6; Gen. 1.27). Here lies the mystery of the Creation Covenant: that life comes forth when *two* unite to become *one*. This is re-affirmed through the marriages of the patriarchs and matriarchs and the children they produce, through the union of Israel and her G-d, and through the unity of *Yeshua* and his assembly. This covenant relationship also extends to the re-unification of the House of Israel and the House of Judah.

> He did this in order to create in union with himself [Messiah] from the two groups a single new humanity… In union with him the whole building is held together, and it is growing into a holy temple in union with the Lord.
>
> (EPH. 2.15B,21)

The union of male and female is described in Scripture as not merely being good but being *tov ma'od* or "very good." *Good* is not used as a casual description of an object or a feeling, but it signifies the fulfillment of function. Together male and female elements are produced after their own kind to populate the earth with the image of G-d. This function was declared *tov ma'od*.

So G-d created Man in His image, in the image of G-d He created him male and female He created them. G-d blessed them and G-d said to them, Be fruitful and multiply, fill the earth...

(GEN. 1.27,28A SCHOTTENSTEIN ED.)

The image of G-d is the form of a house, and mankind producing offspring is to reflect that image. In the ANE, a god who ruled over a particular city took his consort into his temple's inner sanctum to consummate their marriage. The Holy of Holies, called the honeymoon chamber or the couch, was the inner sanctum of G-d's holy temple.

Blow the shofar in Zion; decree a fast; call an assembly; gather the people; summon the congregation; assemble the elders; gather the young children and sucklings; let the bridegroom go forth from his chamber (*chadar*) and the bride from her canopy (*chuppah*).

(JOEL 2.15,16)

The bridal chamber remains hidden behind the curtain. It is the holy in the holy. The veil at first concealed how G-d controlled creation.

(GOSPEL OF PHILIP CG II 3.58,84)

Adam, the first high priest, was created in the image of G-d. Every subsequent high priest represented the unity of male and female when he performed the services inside the Holy of Holies. On *Yom Kippur* (Day of Atonement), the high priest entered the Holy of Holies to restore the relationship between G-d and the community of Israel — thus making *at-one-ment* on behalf of the people. In order to carry out his functions, the high priest had to be married. If his wife died before he performed the services, he married again before entering the Holy of Holies (*Yoma* 1.1). *Yom Kippur*, the day of the final redemption, was the day on which creation was restored, the eternal covenant was permanently established, and unity between heaven and earth was complete.

The Holy of Holies, representing the Sabbath, was described as *Yom Echad* or One Day and was separated from the rest of the house by a veil. The house will be restored when the six days of the creation week re-unite with the seventh day. Restoration will also come when the heavens, which represent the *world to come*, re-unite with the earth: *this world*. Again "the sixth day" is distinguished from the other days by the definite article "the." This is the letter *hey*: the letter that represents the Messianic Kingdom and the same letter added to *Avraham*'s name to make him "the father of many." The purpose of the sixth day was to bring fruitfulness to the world through the unity of Adam and Eve and through the rest of the human race.

According to the book of Jubilees, Moses entered the inner chamber of G-d's Temple atop Mount Sinai. He was told to record the six days of creation and at the same time was given additional details about *Yom Echad*: One Day (details that were omitted from the creation account). British temple scholar Margaret Barker suggests the revelations given to Moses included the secrets of *Yom Echad* — which were the secrets of creation — and the chariot throne of G-d: part of the hidden world behind the curtain inside the Holy of Holies (Jubilees 2.1-3). It was from inside the inner chamber that the past *and* the future of the "six days" were revealed to Moses. According to Barker, this explains why so much history is incorporated into apocalyptic literature. The Books of Revelation and Daniel, for example, record many details about past *and* future events from the perspective of history.

Creation was revealed to Moses as a heavenly prototype that represented, in microcosm, the Temple and the Tabernacle. Jubilees suggests that Moses linked *Yom Echad* to the Tabernacle's exterior frame upon which G-d spread His tent over the beams of creation.

> So Moses raised up the Tabernacle, fastened its sockets, set up its boards, put in its bars, and raised up its pillars. And he spread out the tent over the Tabernacle and put the covering of the tent on top of it, as the Lord had commanded Moses.
>
> (EX. 40:18-19 NKJV)

> Who cover Yourself with light as with a garment, Who stretch out the heavens like a curtain. He lays the beams of His upper chambers in the waters, Who makes the clouds His chariot, Who walks on the wings of the wind.
>
> (PS. 104.2,3 NKJV)

> In them [the heavens] He places a tent for the sun, which comes out like a bridegroom from the bridal chamber.
>
> (PS 19.5B,6A)

Yom Echad or One Day refers to the world outside of time — known only to G-d but sometimes *revealed* to His servants. *Yom Echad* was the reflection of Israel's declaration of faith: Hear *(Shema)* O Israel, the Lord our G-d the Lord is One. *Yom Echad* means that "*Adonai* will be One and His Name will be One" (Zech. 14.9). became a reality in *Yeshua* the Messiah because "unity was both the sign and the proof of divine origin"(Barker 2011: 12).

> I do not pray for these alone, but also for those who will believe in Me through their word; that they all may be one, as You, Father, are in Me, and I in You; that they also may be one in us, that the world may believe that You sent Me.
>
> (JN. 17.20,21 NKJV)

You who at one time were separated from G-d...he has now reconciled in the Son's physical body through his death; in order to present you holy and without defect or reproach before himself...This is the Good News that has been proclaimed in all creation under heaven. The work is to make fully known the message from G-d, the secret hidden for generations, for ages [Olam Hazeh] but now made clear to the people he has set apart for himself. To them G-d wanted to make known how great among the Gentiles is the glorious richness of this secret. And the secret is this: the Messiah is united with you people. In that rests your hope of glory!

(COL. 1.21-23B,25B-27)

The book of Colossians is filled with the rich language of unity, temple building activities, and marriage symbolism. Allusions to creation and the message of *Yom Echad* are found in expressions of oneness linked to Messiah and his community. Paul encourages the Colossians to continue living their lives in unity with Messiah and each other. He explains that it is through their union with Messiah that they have been made full. Finally, he puts all these things in the context of the Good News, that is, to be fruitful in every good work and to multiply in the full knowledge of G-d.

Be Ye Separate from Culture

This know also, that in the last days perilous times shall come. For men shall be lovers of their own selves, covetous, boasters, proud, blasphemers, disobedient to parents, unthankful, unholy, without natural affection, truce-breakers, false accusers, incontinent, fierce, despisers of those that are good, traitors, heady, high-minded, lovers of pleasures more than lovers of G-d; having a form of godliness, but denying the power thereof: from such turn away.

(2 TIM. 3.1–5 KJV)

The Hurrian culture was likely the primary influence on *Avraham* and his family. *Avraham* may have adopted the Hurrian custom in which a wife was known as her husband's sister. This cultural norm could explain why *Avraham* told Pharaoh, under false pretenses, that Sarah *was* his sister. However, many of the choices *Avraham* made likely violated some of the Hurrian's most important customs. The status of landowner, for instance, was the most honorable position in society. When *Avraham* abandoned the family property, it would have brought great shame and humiliation upon his father. It appears Terah lived another sixty years in Charan after *Avraham* left. According to Hurrian traditions, household gods were leased to family members and passed down as part of the dying utterances of a father to his eldest son. *Avraham's* departure before Terah's death meant that he was rejecting his father's household gods — another blow to the family.

The Bible calls us to separate from the culture and to cleave to G-d like *Avraham* did. How do we set ourselves apart and preserve our identity as kingdom citizens when the culture exerts such enormous pressure? No one is immune to its effects. Cultural norms and traditions are strong aphrodisiacs that can seduce even the most upright among us. Men of faith, however, separated themselves from the culture of their day to preserve and protect their family seed. Noah built a boat so his three sons — Shem, Ham, and Japheth — could eventually re-populate the earth. *Avram* left Mesopotamia, "crossed over" to the land of Canaan, confirmed a covenant with G-d, and became *Avraham*: the father of many. Moses led the children of Israel from Egypt's idolatry to the wilderness where they grew into a mighty and powerful nation. Peter gives an encouraging word for facing the cultural giants:

> Dear friends, I urge you as aliens and temporary residents not to give in to the desires of your old nature, which keep

warring against you; but to live such good lives among the pagans that even though they now speak against you as evil doers, they will, as a result of seeing your good actions, give glory to G-d on the Day of His coming.

(1 PETER 2.11,12)

The culture in which one lives may well have the greatest impact on the family. Today, virtually every institution that was once positively influenced by a Judeo-Christian worldview has now been hijacked by the godlessness of secular humanism and the tyranny of political correctness. All society's institutions have been corrupted in some way: the entertainment industry, the arts, media, education, the military, the government, academia, business, and even religion. Today's message is, "anything goes," and "you are *free* to do whatever feels good and works for you — regardless of the consequences."

What happens when a society loses its moral moorings? In its quest to destroy G-d, the left unhitched its wagon from eternal truths and, instead, decided to substitute its own idea of utopia. To reach that utopia — freedom from social expectations and standards — objectivity itself had to be destroyed, so as to avoid blame. Objective truth lost all meaning; only subjectivity mattered…Language became the enemy, since definitions exclude people and things not covered by those definitions; it had to be perverted and hijacked.

(BEN SHAPIRO, THE DAILY WIRE,
FORMER SENIOR EDITOR-AT-LARGE, BREITBART NEWS)

A stable family is the bulwark of society. To the eroding culture, public enemy number one is the father of the house. As the provider, leader, disciplinarian, protector, and defender of the family, a strong father ensures stability in the home. Stable families equal strong societies. Stable families reveal the true nature and character of G-d and reflect His image in the world. Removing the father, marginalizing him, or undermining his authority and purpose leads to the deterioration of the house's foundation. Today's epidemic of fatherless households has contributed to most of society's ills: endless addictions, gang violence, suicides, welfare dependency, the rise in unwed mothers, the murder of unborn babies, and the blight that is the human sex-trafficking industry. The entertainment industry does its fair share of making fathers appear as either bumbling buffoons or sexual predators. This has further contributed to the breakdown of once normal, healthy family relationships where the needs of both sons and daughters were met within the home. Now we find a society of fatherless sons who have been completely lost or forgotten.

The single greatest scourge of our day, however, is the multi-billion dollar, worldwide pornography industry which has as its goal the breakdown of G-d's definition of human sexuality. This has led to the redefinition of marriage and the rise of gender identity issues. Changing the language and making aberrant behavior legitimate won't nullify the disastrous consequences that result from so-called alternate lifestyles. Simply put, pornography destroys the peace, pleasure, and satisfaction of a good marriage. Pornography promotes selfish pleasure as the highest definition of self and demands the sacrifice of many lives in the process. Pornography and its resulting destructive behavior is nothing more than the counterfeit of healthy, sexual relationships in the context of marriage. It produces oceans of misery and broken and shattered lives. This addiction leaves in its wake unhealthy, abusive, and destructive relationships that are virtually impossible to repair. Pornography breeds adultery, pedophilia, prostitution, human trafficking, and now has ignited the so-called gender rights movement. Debasing human sexuality has allowed for the emergence and cultural promotion of alternative lifestyles — further confusing young boys and girls about their own sexuality. Pornography destroys the "traditional" family and has become the gateway drug for all manner of depravity.

Easy access to the Internet, the rise of social media, and the endless use of electronic devices have wreaked havoc in unimaginable ways. Suicide among teens is at an all-time high. Young children are the most vulnerable when it comes to pornography and have often suffered irreparable harm. Destructive, unhealthy images are forever imprinted on their tiny brains. Experts in the field have found that the effects of pornography are not just impacting children but are flooding all corners of society. Pornography has now become a certifiable public health crisis. The porn culture first hyper-sexualizes girls and then exploits them from a very young age. That pornography is now a corrosive cultural norm cannot be overstated.

A dear friend and former porn addict, who once wrote non-professionally on Internet boards, recently shared her experiences with me. She believes porn literally damaged the circuitry of her brain and seriously degraded important connections. "I think I killed them," she said. Her advice to parents is not to assume there is *any* "safe" amount of sexual stimulation to the brain outside the marriage bed.

> I can tell you without hesitation that there are no safe forms of porn that you can be exposed to — be it the romance novels, magazine covers that excite the mind, or movies that combine music and visuals in order to manipulate the pleasure centers. We live with the lie that children can't be poisoned by it unless they are actually being molested. We like to imagine that porn is less destructive to girls than boys, and yet, at eight, I was obsessively drawing pictures in the privacy of my room after exposure to a very raunchy calendar at my father's workplace – even though we had no such pornography

in our own home. Despite being saved at 29, I struggled with obsessive thoughts until I was 33 — four terrible years of being tormented day and night. Deliverance didn't undo the damage to my brain. It was impossible for me to relate to sex in a normal and healthy way. Thirteen years later and I still live with the consequences of pornography and perhaps I always will. Don't get me wrong, being free of the torment of those terrible images is wonderful and I am grateful every day. The first dose of poison was fed to me, but I was the one who kept going back for another taste. There are no safe levels or safe forms of porn — there is no immunity attached just because you are female or because you are young. It is no safer on your mind if you view it at home or at an adult bookstore. Like any other drug, you have no idea which dose will be the addictive dose.

TYLER DAWN ROSENQUIST,
ANCIENT BRIDGE PUBLISHING

These aren't problems that can be easily solved. At times it appears overwhelming and it will clearly take more than "standing on" a few Bible verses to heal the fractured and devastated lives left behind. Parents will have to remain ever vigilant — with each other and with their children. Rebuilding the house can only begin one family at a time. Frank family discussions are absolutely crucial. Learning to distinguish between Biblical principles and cultural norms is essential.

Therefore be imitators of G-d, as beloved children. And walk in love, as Christ loved us and gave himself up for us a fragrant offering and sacrifice to G-d. But sexual immorality and all impurity or covetousness must not even be named among you, as is proper among saints. Let there be no filthiness nor foolish talk nor crude joking, which are out of place, but instead let there be thanksgiving. For you may be sure of this, that everyone who is sexually immoral or impure, or who is covetous, has no inheritance in the kingdom of Christ and G-d. Let no one deceive you with empty words, for because of these things the wrath of G-d comes upon the sons of disobedience. Therefore do not become partners with them; for at one time you were darkness, but now you are light in the Lord. Walk as children of light, and try to discern what is pleasing to the Lord. Take no part in the unfruitful works of darkness, but instead expose them. For it is shameful even to speak of the things that they do in secret.

(EPH. 5.1-12 ESV)

But for those who are willing to *hear* and *obey* G-d's commandments...

He is like a man building a house who dug deep and laid the foundation on the rock. And when the flood arose, the stream beat vehemently against that house, and could not shake it, for it was founded on the rock.

(LUKE 6.48 NKJV)

The Word of G-d is a barometer that measures how far we've strayed from His path. That goes for all behavior related to pornography. His Word is *the* constraint for out of control behavior and a safeguard against moral depravity. We must first face reality then acknowledge the problem and assess the damage. Individually, we can't fix everyone but we can certainly focus like a laser on ourselves and on our families. A family that follows Biblical principles provides a hedge of protection for its members. The Bible is clear that we must teach G-d's word thoroughly to our children — "to speak of them while you sit in your home, while you walk on the way, when you retire and when you arise" (Deut. 6.6,7 Artscroll Stone Ed.).

Rescuing our children from the indoctrination of the "world's education system" is not an option.

We don't have the "luxury" of indulging our fleshly desires anymore and wasting valuable time. We must humble ourselves daily, confess, and repent to G-d. That's just for starters. We also must be willing to ask for help from those we trust in the community. This problem is too big for government agencies, psychologists, and counselors to fix. It has been reported that, in many, many cases, men never do get free from the addiction. We *must* be willing to bear the burdens of others, especially women who have experienced abuse first hand. We must get out of our comfort zones, get our hands dirty, and get in the trenches to help save those held captive and those who have been violated by this deadly enemy.

Whenever a family is healed, restored, and set free, creation comes that much closer to being restored. So model godly behavior in your home — replace evil with good, injustice with G-d's justice, and the enemy's lies with *the* truth. *Clothe yourself with feelings of compassion and with kindness, humility, gentleness and patience* (Col. 3.12,13). BEAR WITH ONE ANOTHER!

CHAPTER FOUR

ATONEMENT AND RESTORATION

He is to take a censer full of burning coals from the altar before Adonai and, with his hands full of ground, fragrant incense, bring it inside the curtain. He is to put the incense on the fire before Adonai, so that the cloud from the incense will cover the ark-cover which is over the testimony, in order that he not die.

(Lev. 16.12,13)

The priests indeed are good but the High Priest is better; to whom the Holy of Holies has been committed and who alone has been trusted with the secrets of G-d. He is the door of the Father by which enter in Abraham, Isaac and Jacob and the prophets and the apostles and the church. All these have for their object the attaining to the Unity of G-d.

(IGNATIUS *Philadelphians* 9)

The following account is not a Midrashic story but rather a depiction of events leading up to and surrounding the incense service conducted by the high priest on the Day of Atonement. This account is based on material from Leviticus (16) and the tractate *Yoma* in the Mishnah which contains the best information about the service.

High Priest *Yehoshua* Ben David reflected on the previous week's preparations for *Yom Kippur* (Day of Atonement). He had left his family compound in the city of Jerusalem in order to sequester himself in the *Palhedrin* chamber of the *Azarah*: the inner courtyard of the Temple complex. Seven days of consecration were required to achieve the highest level of ritual purity — necessary for performing the service on this holy day. Separated from his wife and family, he would not become *tamai* (ritually impure). As a safeguard, another priest had been prepared to perform the *Yom Kippur* services should he become disqualified; *Yehoshua* was determined that would not happen.

During the six days leading up to *Yom Kippur*, *Yehoshua* had taken great pleasure in performing the required temple duties: sprinkling the blood from the morning and evening offerings, burning the incense on the golden altar, and dressing the seven-branched menorah — adding new wicks and freshly pressed oil and even lighting the lamps. *Yehoshua* had been sprinkled with the water and ash mixture from the burnt red heifer in order to maintain ritual purity throughout the week. The Elders of the Court had spent hours in his chamber each day — teaching him the laws of the service. An unpretentious chamber by temple standards, the *Palhedrin* was sparsely furnished with only a small bed, several wooden chairs, and a plain wooden table. Evening visits with the elders had been especially satisfying. Lively debates ensued as they studied the service from *Acharei Mot* (After Death, Lev. 16): the Torah portion for *Yom Kippur*. For *Yehoshua*, the incense service would be the highlight of the day. Understanding that he would represent the entire nation, and that he would stand between the dead and the living, caused him a certain amount of anxiety. Haunted by the responsibility set before him, *Yehoshua* fell on his face before G-d in an attitude of thanksgiving — grateful for having been chosen to serve as High Priest.

On the morning of *Yom Kippur* eve, *Yehoshua* joined the Elders of the Court at the Eastern Gate. He took time to scrutinize each of the animals chosen for the day's offerings; oxen, rams, and sheep were paraded before him as he nodded his approval. Then he made his way, along with some of the Elders of the Court, to the upper chamber of *Bet Avtinas* to oversee final preparations for the *ketoret* (incense). The spice compound was ground a second time resulting in a very fine powder. The grinding left a heavenly aroma lingering in the air — saturating *Yehoshua's* garments and permeating the entire Temple complex. *Yehoshua* would return to the *Avtinas* chamber for final instructions before handling the *ketoret*.

As darkness descended, all food and drink was removed from the High Priest's chamber. *Yehoshua* was required to stay awake, and eating and drinking would only induce drowsiness. The elders joined him in his chamber once again — this time to make sure he did not fall asleep. Periodically, they would sing out loud from the Book of Psalms. When *Yehoshua* felt himself nodding off, he would abruptly shake his head and then gently slap his cheeks. One young priest, slightly hesitant at first, loudly snapped his fingers when *Yehoshua* began to doze; another politely asked the High Priest to stand. When *Yehoshua's* feet hit the cold, marble, chamber floor, the shock forced him wide-awake. No footwear was ever worn in the holy precincts. It was said that when the High Priest's feet came in contact with the floor, this symbolized the manifestation of the Divine Presence in the sacred precincts. All night the men studied together — expounding on a variety of legal topics — reading from the books of Job, Ezra, and Chronicles.

Dawn's light cast its first rays through the window of the

chamber, and the High Priest, weary from standing most of the night, let out a sigh of relief. The day had finally arrived and with it a tinge of excitement accompanied by a few butterflies. He could not make any mistakes today. As the eastern sky lit up over Hebron, and just before the ritual slaughterings began, *Yehoshua* was led downstairs to the *mikvah* (immersion bath) for the first of five immersions. Once he'd bathed and dried, he carefully donned his priestly attire for the regular morning services. The eight articles were called the "golden garment," and they matched *the parokhet* (curtain) in front of the Holy of Holies. His garments were woven with *techelet*: wool dyed sky-blue from the hilazon sea mollusk, *argamon*: wool dyed purple, *tolat sheni*: wool dyed dark red from a worm, and *shesh*: white linen. Each color represented elements from the material world.

After each ritual immersion, *Yehoshua* would change his clothes — alternating between his golden and his white garments. The golden garments were worn for the outer service: the regular morning and afternoon offerings. The white garments were worn for the inner service: the confessions, the casting of lots for the two goats, the sprinkling of the blood and the burning of the incense inside the Holy of Holies, and finally the removal of the firepan from the inner chamber. After the regular morning service was completed, *Yehoshua* followed the elders to a *mikvah* on the roof of the *Bet Haparvah* (house of the tanning) chamber. They held up a linen sheet to shield him from the people as he performed his second immersion. After quickly drying himself with the same sheet, *Yehoshua* dressed in white linen garments made from the beaten stalk of the flax plant. The four garments — a tunic, pants, belt, and turban — were always worn by the High Priest when performing the *Yom Kippur* services. By wearing these *pelusium* (white garments of fine linen), he would be dressed like the angels as he passed through the curtain to the heavenly realm. Inside the Holy of Holies, the High Priest would no longer be the "human emissary" but would become part of the heavenly angelic host. The white garments he wore that day would never be worn again.

Yehoshua made his way to the north end of the Temple courtyard between the porch and the great altar where a young bull stood ready to be slaughtered. The head of the bull was turned so that he faced west towards the holy sanctuary. *Yehoshua*, with his back facing east, placed his hands between the bull's horns and made the confession:

I have done wrong, I have transgressed, I have sinned before You, I and my house...for on this day shall atonement be made for you, to cleanse you, from all your sins shall you be clean before the Lord.

Then he said a prayer for himself and for his own family, and he spoke the unpronounceable *Shem HaMeforash*: the ineffable name. When they heard the Name, the crowd of worshippers who had gathered to witness the service of the High Priest fell on their faces and cried out in unison, "*Baruch Shem Kevod Malchuto Le'olam Va'ed*: Blessed be the Name of His glorious kingdom forever and ever!" After receiving the blood of the bull, it was time for the High Priest to offer the incense.

Yehoshua ascended the middle of the ramp to the great altar. Normally four woodpiles burned on the altar each day, but on *Yom Kippur* an additional pile was added from which the High Priest would take the coals for the incense service. He pushed the smoldering coals aside so he could scoop the glowing coals, and his golden firepan flushed red. Carrying the firepan filled with coals, *Yehoshua* made his way back down the altar ramp to the Temple courtyard. There another priest stood stirring the blood of the slaughtered bull so it would not congeal. The marble pavement stone of the courtyard was laid in rows, and each row was called a terrace. It was at the fourth terrace that *Yehoshua* waited for the priests to bring him the golden ladle from the chamber of the vessels and a pan filled with finely ground incense from the *Bet Avtinas*.

With the heavier golden firepan in his right hand and the lighter golden ladle with the incense in his left hand, *Yehoshua* focused carefully on not dropping either the incense or the coals. He had trained for this moment for nearly a year; any spilled grains would be disastrous for the nation. It required great dexterity and good balance to maneuver the incense, the coals, and the vessels.

The High Priest moved slowly and deliberately up the twelve steps into the *ulam* (porch) and towards the inner sanctuary of the Temple. As he approached the Holy of Holies, he stopped for a moment to admire the curtain's intricate weave in vibrant blue, red, and purple. The outer curtain had been fastened with a golden clasp. Its top was folded towards the outside to create a southern entryway. The inner curtain was fastened on the northern side. *Yehoshua* walked between the curtain parallels that now formed a hallway. As he passed through the veils, he saw the divine light appear from the cube-shaped room that was lined with pure gold. His heart pounding, he tried to steady his emotions. He was filled with a sense of awe and wonder at the majesty and splendor before him. There simply weren't words to describe what he saw. *Yehoshua* found it difficult even to move his feet forward as the glory of G-d pressed in all around him. He stood mesmerized by the two monumental figures of the cherubim — each with the body of a winged animal and the head of a man. They appeared to be frozen in time — their wingtips reaching out to touch one another. The golden Ark of the Testimony sat under the massive wingspan to form a chariot throne for the King of the Universe. *Yehoshua* took his position between the two poles that jutted from the sides of the Ark towards the curtains.

The High Priest placed the firepan on the *even shetiyah*: the great stone. The stone was slightly higher than the ground, and it served as the foundation of the house. Deftly, *Yehoshua* maneuvered the incense into his hands and then heaped the handful onto the coals — side-stepping to avoid being burned.

This was the most difficult task of any in the Temple for it required great expertise and much practice. As he took a step back, *Yehoshua's* eyes widened as he felt the heat from the burning coals. He waited anxiously for the entire chamber to fill with smoke and for the sweet aroma of the spices to permeate the sacred space. The smoke rose from the Temple as one straight column. A secret ingredient, called the *ma'aleh ashan* (smoke riser) and known only to the members of the House of *Avtinas*, was said to cause the smoke to ascend like a pillar. The herb had no fragrance, but it did prevent the heavy smoke from burning *Yehoshua's* eyes. As he gazed upon the pillar of smoke, he couldn't help but compare this sight with the pillar of cloud that protected Israel as they traveled through the wilderness.

Yehoshua saw the glory hovering over the Ark of the Covenant just as the Spirit of G-d had hovered over the primordial waters at creation. It was through the *ketoret* that the *Shekinah* (indwelling presence) would rest upon Israel. *Yehoshua* was overwhelmed by the sense that he was standing in the center of eternity and that the incense service was a remembrance of the *Brit Esh*: the Covenant of Fire. It signified the restoration of the created order through atonement. The *ketoret* not only restored the bond between G-d and man, but it brought unity to all of Israel.

The High Priest kept his face fixed towards the Ark of the Covenant as he moved backwards to exit the Holy of Holies. He said a short prayer as he passed back through the curtain, and a shiver ran down his spine. The wonder and majesty of the moment did not escape him. He had met with the G-d of the Universe — face-to-face in a cloud — and he had lived.

Day of Atonement

> *It is to be a permanent regulation for you that on the tenth day of the seventh month you are to deny yourselves and not*

do any kind of work, both the citizens and the foreigner living with you. For on this day, atonement will be made for you to purify you; you will be clean before Adonai from all your sins. It is a Shabbat of complete rest for you, and you are to deny yourselves.

(LEV. 16.29-31)

G-d created the world through the *Brit Esh* (Covenant of Fire): an eternal covenant that was designed to keep and maintain an ordered universe. "A broken Creation Covenant brought the wrath and so repairing the breach in the covenant was called atonement" (Barker 2010: 123). Sin broke the bonds of the covenant, so renewing the eternal covenant required atonement. The Temple services for *Yom Kippur* (Day of Atonement) were annual re-creation rituals designed to repair the breach and to commemorate the restoration of *Yom Echad* or One Day: creation's original state. The sprinkling of blood and the burning of incense in the Holy of Holies were atonement rituals that protected the people from G-d's wrath. But in reality, the creation was only symbolically restored through these services.

Anciently, *Yom Kippur* was a joyous occasion that celebrated not only the Jubilee Year (the fiftieth year following seven sabbatical years which provided a release from all debts) but also the annual New Year's festival. It was a day for rejoicing when the high priest emerged unscathed from the inner sanctum. It was a day marked by feasting and marriages — not self-denial. "Surely the day that heralded this 'year of liberty' was a day of unbridled joy," for it was the day "the daughters of Jerusalem went forth to dance in the vineyards" (J. Milgrom 2004: 162-63). By the Second Temple period, *Yom Kippur* had become the solemn assembly it is today with its emphasis on asceticism. As part of the annual New Year's festival, it was recognized as a day of judgment and redemption: a time when sins were either atoned for or punished. Judging human behavior was key to maintaining the created order.

On this day, the high priest emptied himself of all impurity in order to personally perform the services — thus purifying the people and the Temple. "The rituals of the Day of Atonement were the annual means by which the mediator was enabled to enter, briefly, the divine presence in the Holy of Holies and thereby effect a temporary restoration of the creation to purity and wholeness" (Barker 2008: 44).

Yom HaKippurim should be translated as "the day of the atonements." *Kippur* comes from the root *kappar*, meaning cover, and suggests some kind of protective covering. A similar word appears in Exodus 16 in the description of the manna under the dew: "something thin like *k'por* (frost) covering the surface of the wilderness." *Kapporet*, which is the cover over the Ark of the Covenant, has been incorrectly referred to as the mercy seat (Martin Luther translated it "mercy seat"). Jacob Milgrom proposed that *kappar* could also mean "to wipe" and that *kapporet* is not really translatable. He explains it as "a solid gold slab atop the ark, at the edges of which were two cherubim, of one piece with it made of hammered gold, kneeling and facing each other with bowed heads and outstretched wings so as to touch in the middle" (2004: 167).

The Hebrew letters in *kapporet* (cover) can be rearranged to form *parokhet* (curtain). The curtain and the cover are the two places on which the high priest sprinkled the blood. The gematria or numerical value (letters in a word or a phrase are given a meaning based on a number value) of these words is 700: a temple number related to the seventh day, the Holy of Holies, the Kingdom, and the restoration of creation (discussed in chapter 6). *Kapporet* is also mentioned seven times in the Torah portion that outlines the atonement rituals for *Yom Kippur* (Lev 16). The atonement service is likely explained here in response to the death of Aaron's two sons, Nadab and Abihu, several chapters earlier. After putting coals in their firepans and laying incense on top, Aaron's sons drew near to G-d with "strange fire." The Hebrew word for strange fire is *zur: to* spread or scatter as a stranger who is scattered abroad. *Zur* can also mean, however, "one who is estranged" or even "a harlot." This suggests that Aaron's sons broke the intimate covenant relationship with G-d by their actions. Covenants were relational, so when a covenant was broken it resulted in an estranged relationship between the two parties. In the case of Aaron's sons, the hedge of protection that the covenant provided was removed, and they were judged with death for their disobedience.

On *Yom Kippur,* the high priest offered up a total of fifteen animal sacrifices; fifteen is a number associated with the highest form of worship and entering the Divine Presence. He chose two goats by lot: one dedicated to the Lord and the other sent to its death in the wilderness. On both the *kapporet* and the *parokhet,* he sprinkled the blood of a bull that he offered up for himself and his family. This same bull's blood would later be mixed with the blood of the goat that the high priest offered to the Lord. A second time, this blood would be sprinkled on the *kapporet* and the *parokhet.* There was no ark in the Holy of Holies of the Second Temple, so the high priest sprinkled the blood in the air seven times with his finger — like a whip — imagery that conveyed an act of cleansing. (*Yeshua* took a whip (Jn. 2.15) and drove out the moneychangers to cleanse the Temple before Passover.) The high priest also sprinkled the blood on the four corners of the golden altar of incense (inside the Holy Place) and on the great altar which stood in front of the Temple building. The remaining blood he poured under the altar — symbolic of the souls of the martyrs who cry out (Rev. 6.9,10), "How long until you judge and avenge our blood?" Blood was *the* symbol of life, and it contained purifying properties capable of cleansing from the contamination of sin. Therefore, atonement through blood brought life to the creation.

G-d's design for the *permanent* restoration of creation

was through the shed blood of His Son, *Yeshua* the Messiah. Atonement was not required to appease an angry G-d but rather to remove the effects of human sin and to repair the broken covenant. In her article, "Atonement in Leviticus," Mary Douglas defines atonement:

> ...to cover or recover, repair a hole, cure a sickness, mend a rift, make good a torn or broken covering. Atonement does not mean covering a sin so as to hide it from the sight of G-d; it means making good an outer layer which has been rotted or pierced.
>
> (JEWISH STUDIES QUARTERLY 1 1993-4: 117)

Yeshua's own blood was sprinkled upon the Ark of the Covenant in the heavenly Holy of Holies: the world outside of time. His blood restored creation and rebuilt the covenant bond between G-d and man. "He is the bond of our wholeness and by his uniting us we are healed" (Is. 53.5 Barker's translation).

> But Christ came as High Priest of the good things to come, with the greater and more perfect tabernacle not made with hands, that is, not of this creation. Not with the blood of goats and calves, but with His own blood He entered the Most Holy Place once for all, having obtained eternal redemption.
>
> (HEBREWS 9.11,12 NKJV)

When *Yeshua* said, "For this is my blood of the New Covenant, which is shed for many for the remission of sins" (Matt 26.28 NKJV), he knew his atonement would lead to the permanent restoration of creation as it was in the beginning. Many see his atonement as the "New Covenant" which replaced an "old covenant" that had become obsolete. However, his shed blood *renewed* the Creation Covenant (called the "New

Covenant") to restore the original — not to replace it. It was broken because of sin and re-instated by blood. It seems the word "new" was a later addition to the wording in the New Testament; "New Covenant" did not appear until the Greek texts Codex Alexandrinus and Codex Bezae in the fifth century (Barker 2007: 177).

When the covenant bond was broken through sin and rebellion, the protection the covenant afforded was removed and G-d's wrath was poured out upon the people. The prophets continually warned the nation that their sin, especially regarding their treatment of the House of G-d, was causing the natural order to collapse. Haggai (1.7-11) said that neglect of G-d's House would bring severe drought and famine. The land of Israel and the Temple were inextricably tied to the state of the Creation Covenant.

> The land lies defiled under its inhabitants; because they have transgressed the teachings, changed the law and broken the everlasting covenant. Therefore a curse is devouring the land, and its inhabitants are punished for their guilt...the city of chaos is shattered, every house closed up; no one can enter. In the streets they are crying over the wine; all joy has faded, cheer has left the land. In the city, only desolation, its gates are battered beyond repair.
>
> (IS. 24.5-6,10-12)

The book of Revelation is filled with cataclysmic signs: the sun darkened, the moon not giving light, stars falling from heaven, and the powers shaken to describe a Day of Wrath. These signs were related to the Temple. As a consequence for breaking His covenant, the Temple in Jerusalem would be destroyed by the Romans in 70 CE, and Israel would be sent into exile. Creation out of balance resulted in all kinds of natural disasters: earthquakes, famine, pestilence, crop failure, and cosmic upheavals that were poured out upon the earth in the context of the Day of the Lord. Philo said, "The world is in harmony with the Law and the Law with the world and so breaking the Law affected the creation" (Quoted in Barker 2010: 153).

In His fierce anger He cut off all the power of Israel, withdrew His protecting right hand at the approach of the enemy...in the tent of the daughter of *Tziyon* He poured out His fury like fire. He wrecked His Tabernacle as easily as a garden, destroyed His place of assembly. *Adonai* caused Israel to forget designated times and *Shabbats*. In the heat of His anger He rejected both king and *Kohen*.

(LAM. 2.3,4B,6)

Part of the *Shema* (Hear O Israel, the Lord our G-d, the Lord is One...) describes the wrath that G-d will pour out for disobeying His commandments:

Beware lest your heart be seduced and you turn astray and serve gods of others and bow to them. Then the wrath of *HaShem* will blaze against you. He will restrain the heaven so there will be no rain and the ground will not yield its produce. And you will be swiftly banished from the goodly land, which *Hashem* gives you.

(DEUT. 11.16,17 ARTSCROLL SIDDUR)

In the story of Korah's rebellion when wrath threatened the people, Aaron, the high priest, offered the incense for atonement. He stood between the dead and the living, and the plague stopped. The high priest would later offer incense inside the Holy of Holies of the Temple as a ritual act of atonement.

Moshe said to *Aharon*, Take your fire pan, put fire from the altar in it, lay incense on it and hurry with it to the assembly to make atonement for them, because anger has gone out from *Adonai* and the plague has already begun! *Aharon* took it, as *Moshe* had said and ran to the middle of the assembly. There the plague had already begun among the people, but he added the incense and made atonement for the people. He stood between the dead and the living, and the plague was stopped.

(NUM. 17.11-13)

Symbolically, the service of the blood and the incense that were performed by the high priest on *Yom Kippur* temporarily provided the atonement necessary to prevent the destructive consequences of wrath and judgment. Messiah's atonement, however, permanently repaired the breach and reversed the collapsing covenant. So, just as the high priest carried the iniquity of those he atoned for, Messiah bore the iniquity of all our sins in order to restore the broken Creation Covenant forever.

The Incense Cloud

He shall place the incense upon the fire before the Lord so as to cover with the cloud of the incense the ark cover that is atop the testimony so that he not die.

(LEV. 16.12B)

Like cassia and camel thorn I gave forth the aroma of spices and like choice myrrh I spread a pleasant odor like galbanum, onycha and stacte and like the fragrance of frankincense in the tabernacle.

(SIRACH 24.15)

We generally assume the blood sprinkled in the Holy of Holies at *Yom Kippur* was the only atonement ritual, but the incense service also provided atonement. When the incense was laid upon the fiery coals, a cloud of smoke rose to fill the inner chamber and cover the Ark of the Covenant. This ritual foreshadowed the return of the *Shekinah* (the Glory of G-d) to His house and the restoration of the broken *Brit Esh* (Covenant of Fire). The *ketoret* (incense) acted as a covering for the nation to protect from the divine wrath of G-d. The cloud hid the throne and so shielded the high priest from the divine presence. This shield was necessary because mortal flesh cannot stand "face-to-face" (idiom for *Yom Kippur*) with the Creator and live.

Ketoret (incense) means bonding. The offering of incense created the bond needed to repair the Creation Covenant. *Ketoret* symbolized unity. The individual spices became one sweet-smelling aroma — a picture of the redeemed of the Lord. *Rashi* compared the eleven ingredients to the unity of the congregation. He said that the eleventh ingredient, the *ma'aleh ashan* (smoke rising herb), represented the sinner who united with the congregation as a whole (represented by the ten ingredients). The *ma'aleh ashan* caused the smoke from the incense to ascend in a straight, pillar-like column.

For the Tabernacle services, four spices were compounded: frankincense, stacte, onycha, and galbanum (Ex. 30.34,35). Philo connected these four spices to the four natural elements (earth, air, fire, and water) "out of which the whole world was brought to completion" (*Who is Heir?* 197). The foul-smelling galbanum acquired a sweet fragrance when mixed with the other three spices. Hence galbanum was compared to the wicked whose "smell" is transformed by the sweet scent of the righteous. Josephus lists thirteen sweet-smelling spices (*Wars of the Jews* 5.218), and the Talmud (BT *Keriot* 6a; Yerushalmi *Yoma* 4.5) lists eleven spices including a minute amount of the *ma'aleh ashan*. Added to this mixture were Sodom salt, lye, and Cyprus wine. The eleven spices were compounded according to a secret formula that was passed down through the family of *Avtinas*. They were responsible for making the incense for the Second Temple. The incense was burned twice a day (during the regular morning and afternoon services) as well as on *Yom Kippur*. Once every sixty or seventy years, an additional portion — the size of the high priest's hands — was set aside. When collected it provided half the year's supply of incense.

Each year the *Kohanim* (priests from *Bet Avtinas*) made enough *ketoret* to provide one portion per day for the regular incense service and three additional portions for the *Yom Kippur* service. The high priest "filled both hands," a sign of his priesthood, when he offered up the portion of incense.

> And then his kingdom shall appear throughout all his creation, and then Satan shall be no more, and sorrow shall depart with him. Then the *hands of the angel shall be filled* who has been appointed chief, and he shall forthwith avenge them of their enemies. For the Heavenly One will arise from His royal throne, And he will go forth from His Holy Habitation with indignation and wrath on account of his sons. And the earth shall tremble: to its confines shall be shaken: And the high mountains shall be made low, and the hills shall be shaken and fall.
>
> (ASSUMPTION OF MOSES 10.1-4)

A unique property of the *ketoret* was that it atoned for *lashon harah* (evil tongue) or disparaging speech against others. According to Rabbi Culi in his commentary *Ma'om Lo'ez*, "the incense was an enlightened remedy to purify from sin — so that whoever smelled the incense as it burned on the golden altar of incense would have thoughts of repentance." This resulted in a heart that was purified from evil thoughts and evil speech.

> And he [the high priest] shall have made atonement for himself, and for his household, and for all the assembly of the house of Israel. What atonement is there which

obtains evenly for himself, his household, his brethren, the priests, and the whole assembly of the house of Israel? It is the smoking of the incense. But does the incense obtain atonement? Indeed, for R. *Hananiah* cited: We learn that the incense obtains *atonement for what was said*: And he put on the incense and made atonement for the people.

(BT Yoma 44A)

This helps to explain Isaiah's vision in the heavenly throne room (Is 6.1-7). Isaiah's vision is written in language that conveys atonement: He sees G-d sitting on a high and lofty throne with the hem of His robe filling the Temple. He sees the six-winged *Seraphim* (burning) standing over the throne and crying out to one another, "*Kadosh, kadosh, kadosh* (Holy, holy, holy) is *Adonai Tzva'ot* (Lord of Hosts). The whole earth is filled with His glory." He sees the doorposts shake, and he watches as the Temple is filled with the smoke cloud from the incense. The scene is similar to what Israel saw when receiving the Torah on the mountain (Ex. 19.18). Mount Sinai was enveloped in smoke when G-d descended on it in fire; its smoke went up like the smoke from a furnace and the whole mountain shook violently.

> Then I said, Woe is me I am doomed: for I am a man of impure lips and I dwell among a people with impure lips, for my eyes have seen the King, *HaShem*, Master of Legions. One of the Seraphim flew to me and in his hand was a coal; he had taken it with tongs from atop the altar. He touched it to my mouth and said, Behold, this has touched your lips; your iniquity has gone away and your sin shall be atoned for.

(IS. 6.5,6 ARTSCROLL STONE ED.)

One possibility as to why Moses was forbidden to enter the land may have to do with the incense service. Moses was commanded to speak to "the rock" in order to receive water for the community (Num. 20.7-12). The rock was a picture of the oracle of G-d, the *debir* (to speak: a name for the Holy of Holies), where G-d spoke to Moses. Moses struck the rock twice with his staff — instead of speaking to it — and water flowed out immediately. Legend has it that *this* rock came from the foundation stone atop Mount Moriah where the world received its water. This rock was said to have followed the children of Israel throughout their wilderness wanderings — resting inside the Tabernacle whenever they camped. In the Temple service on *Yom Kippur*, the high priest placed the incense on this same rock.

The Hebrew word for strike, *nach*, is formed from two letters: *nun* and *kaf*. *Nun* means seed, and *kaf* is a palm. The ladle for the incense was also called a *kaf* because from it the high priest would take the incense and put it into his palm. *Nach* means "something crushed" as in seed finely ground to powder. Were the crushed seeds the *ketoret* in the palm of his hand? Could Moses have been acting as mediator to provide atonement for the community? Was Moses "cut off" because of their ongoing grumbling, complaining, and speaking against the leadership: *lashon harah*? Was he, metaphorically speaking, the righteous one who atoned for their sin, "died" on their behalf, and suffered the consequences?

When Moses ascended to receive the tablets of stone, the Glory of G-d covered the mountain like a cloud. The Glory remained for six days, and on the seventh day G-d called Moses out from that cloud. In the Temple, as the high priest waited for the incense to fill the inner chamber and cover the ark, he also became enveloped in a *cloud of glory* (Ex. 24.18). "For in a cloud I shall be seen on the *kapporet*" (Lev. 16.2 Artscroll Stone Ed.).

Then I looked, and suddenly, on the dome over the heads of the *K'ruvim* (cherubim), there appeared above them something like sapphire that seemd to take the form of a throne. He spoke to the man clothed in linen...Go in between the wheels under the *K'ruvim*, fill both your hands with fiery coals from between the *K'ruvim* and throw them on the city...Now the cherubim were standing to the right of the house when the man entered, and the cloud filled the inner courtyard. The glory of *Adonai* rose from above the *Keruv* to the threshold of the house, leaving the house filled with the cloud and the courtyard full of the brilliance of *Adonai's* glory.

(EZEK. 10.1-4)

A Jewish tale (from Pesikta *Rabbati* 20:4) tells of Moses's ascent to the top of the mountain. As he reached the summit, he saw a floating cloud that opened as he approached. He stepped inside and found himself in the presence of a great light. The cloud took him up to heaven, and when he reached the gates of the firmament the cloud again opened; he stepped up into Paradise where he stood before the Throne of G-d. There he saw G-d weaving crowns from the letters of the Torah. The angels questioned Him about giving the treasure of the Torah to a man, but the Holy One replied that the Torah was created for that purpose (Schwartz, 1993: 45-47).

The cloud foreshadowed *Yeshua's* role as mediator of the Creation Covenant and protector from the wrath of G-d. The sages declared, "*Ananei* (He of the clouds) is King Messiah who will in the future reveal himself " (Targum: 1 Chron. 3:24). Second Temple period literature describes Messiah as "this Man" who "flew with the clouds of heaven" (4 Ezra 13.3). The sages identified two distinct time frames when Messiah would appear: "If they will be righteous, the Messiah will come on the clouds of heaven; if they will not be righteous he will come as a poor man riding on a donkey" (BT *Sanhedrin* 98a).

This is the backdrop for the "transfiguration" (Matt. 17.1-8): a word that means "resplendent with divine brightness."

Yeshua's face shone like the sun — like Moses's when he was face-to-face with G-d. *Yeshua's* clothing became as white as light — like the high priest's garment on *Yom Kippur*.

> While he was still speaking, behold, a bright cloud overshadowed them; and suddenly a voice came out of the cloud, saying, "This is my beloved Son, in whom I am well pleased. Hear Him!"
>
> (MATT. 17.5 NKJV)

> Then I looked, and there before me was a white cloud. Sitting on the cloud was someone like a Son of Man with a gold crown on his head and a sharp sickle in his hand.
>
> (REV. 14.14)

> How glorious was he when he looked forth from the Tent, and when he came out of the sanctuary! Like a morning star from between the clouds, and like full moon on the feast days; like the sun shining upon the Temple of the Most High, and like the rainbow becoming visible in the cloud...when he put on his glorious robes, and clothed himself in perfect splendor.
>
> (SIRACH 50.5-7,11)

In his vision, Daniel describes the throne room (Dan. 7.9-14) as fiery flames with wheels of burning fire and a stream of fire flowing from the presence of the Ancient of Days. He saw one like a Son of Man coming with the clouds of heaven to approach the Ancient of Days. The Son of Man was given rulership, glory, and a kingdom. Understanding that the cloud is the incense smoke in the Holy of Holies should help clarify a familiar verse in the Book of Acts:

After saying this, he was taken up before their eyes; and a cloud hid him from their sight...This *Yeshua* who has been taken away from you into heaven, will come back to you in just the same way as you saw him go into heaven.

(ACTS 1.9,11)

The framework for the book of Revelation should be examined from the perspective of *Yom Kippur*. The angel who receives the incense is *the* High Priest, *Yeshua* the Messiah, the Son of Man. He is wearing a robe down to his feet (a *ketonet* or garment of a priest) and a gold band around his chest (Rev 1.13). When his blood is sprinkled over the *kapporet* and on the *parokhet* (curtain), atonement is complete. When the seventh seal is opened, an angel stands at the golden altar with a large quantity of incense. The incense is the covering for G-d's wrath, and the rising smoke is the cloud that enwraps the angel/high priest.

> *Afterwards* (Barker's translation), the angel came and stood at the altar with a gold incense bowl, and he was given a large quantity of incense to add to the prayers of all G-d's people on the gold altar in front of the throne. The smoke of the incense went up with the prayers of G-d's people from the hand of the angel before G-d. Then the angel took the incense bowl, filled it with fire from the altar and threw it down onto the earth and there followed peals of thunder, voices, flashes of lightning, and an earthquake.

(REV 8.3)

This describes the final *Yom Kippur* and *Yeshua's* return to the earth. Having first been enthroned in the Holy of Holies, represented by the cloud, Messiah now emerges to judge the earth, destroy G-d's enemies, and restore the broken Creation Covenant.

Next I saw another mighty angel coming down from heaven. He was dressed in a cloud, with a rainbow over his head; his face was like the sun, his legs like columns of fire; and he had a little scroll lying open in his hand. He planted his right foot on the sea and his left foot on the land...

(REV 10.1,2)

Then I looked, and there before me was a white cloud. Sitting on the cloud was someone like a Son of Man with a gold crown on his head and a sharp sickle in his hand.

(REV 14.14)

A similar theme appears in the account of Korah's rebellion against Moses and Aaron (Num. 17). Moses instructed Korah and his men to take their fire-pots with the burning coals and to add incense to prove whether or not they were worthy to approach G-d in His holy sphere. The rebellious men assembled at the entrance to the Tent of Meeting; Moses and Aaron separated themselves from the unholy assembly, and G-d prepared to destroy all 250 rebels with a plague. Judgment began at the entrance to G-d's House for the sin of *lashon harah* (evil tongue). "*Aharon* took it as *Moshe* had said, and ran into the midst of the assembly. There the plague had begun among the people, but he added the incense and made atonement for the people" (Num. 17.12-13).

I looked and the sanctuary (that is the Tent of Witness in heaven) was opened, and out of the sanctuary came seven angels with seven plagues. They were dressed in clean bright linen and had gold belts around their chests. One of the four living beings gave to the seven angels seven gold bowls filled with the fury of G-d, who lives forever and ever. Then the sanctuary was filled with smoke from

G-d's *Shekinah*, that is, from his power; and no one could enter the sanctuary until the seven plagues of the seven angels had accomplished their purpose.

(REV. 15.5-8)

In the Second Temple, prayer accompanied every offering and ritual. It was an integral part of the regular incense service as well as the incense service for *Yom Kippur*. The agents of the people (the *ma'amad* or standing ones) stood, prayed, and observed all of the offerings. *Rambam* said that the intent of the standing ones was "involvement in the Divine service and prayer." They prayed the sacrifices would be acceptable to G-d. The *ma'amad* who were not serving in the Temple during a particular week, or who were too far from Jerusalem to participate, would gather in their local synagogues to pray at the offering times. "Their gathering together for each of these prayers of these four services and their standing in prayer, supplication, and petition and reading the Torah is called a *ma'amad*" (Mishnah Torah, *Sefer Avodah, Klei Hamikdash* ch. 6).

The praise of incense, and true prayer, his holiness atones for our sins. An inside of linen, an arrangement of stones, he was girded with them all like a serving angel.

(EXCERPT FROM A POEM FOR *Yom Kippur*, MA'OM LO'EZ)

One time *Z'kharyah* (Zechariah) was fulfilling his duties as *Kohen* during his division's period (course of the *ma'amad*) of service before G-d, he was chosen by lot (according to the custom among the *Kohanim*) to enter the Temple and burn incense. All the people were outside, praying, at the time of the incense burning, when there appeared to him an angel of *Adonai* standing to the right of the incense altar.

(LUKE 1.8-10)

Our High Priest *Yeshua* provided atonement. He sprinkled his own blood on the *kapporet* and the *parokhet* in the heavenly Holy of Holies. He filled his own hands with cloud-producing incense to protect us from the consequences of a broken covenant. He will re-emerge from the Holy of Holies to judge the world — not only for shedding the blood of his martyrs but for all the unrighteousness and injustice done to his people. The appointed hour draws near, and so our only response should be to repent — the Kingdom of Heaven is in our midst!

✡   ✡   ✡

Vendyl Jones was a famed explorer, an amateur archaeologist, and quite possibly the inspiration for "Indiana Jones: Raiders of the Lost Ark." In April 1992, Vendyl discovered a reddish-brown organic material sealed inside a rock silo in a section of the Qumran cave complex. Test results suggested the compound was a mixture of eight or nine of the eleven spices used in the *ketoret* of the Second Temple. Jones reported that even his hair and clothing retained the fragrant aroma for several days after the discovery. Two additional inorganic materials were found close by in the same cave: Karsina Lye and Sodom salt. The substance was later analyzed by the Weizmann Institute of Science as well as by two departments at Bar-Ilan University in Israel. Over 600 pounds of the powder were eventually removed from the cave. Critics, however, continue to claim it was just dirt.

✡   ✡   ✡

The Holy of Holies

The Holy of Holies represented eternity where G-d was enthroned in the midst of His creation. From His throne, light spread to the four corners of the world. Even the windows in the Temple were constructed wide on the inside and narrow on the outside so light could radiate outwards (1 Kings 6.4).

Although the Holy of Holies sat empty in the Second Temple, it is said that "in the time of the Messiah the furnishings missing from the [Holy of Holies] in the Second Temple will be restored: the ark, the fire (incense), the cherubim, the Spirit and the menorah" (Barker 2011: 99). These furnishings all connect to the light of *Yom Echad*: One Day.

> I saw no temple in the city for *Adonai*, G-d of heaven's armies, is its temple, as is the Lamb. The city has no need for the sun or the moon to shine on it because G-d's *Shekinah* (indwelling presence) gives it light, and its lamp is the Lamb.
>
> (REV. 21.22,23)

Yom Echad (One Day), the New Jerusalem, and the Holy of Holies are all synonymous terms. In Solomon's Temple, the Holy of Holies was constructed as a cube — twenty cubits in length, width, and height all overlaid with gold. Therefore, it is likely not coincidental that John's description of the heavenly city, the New Jerusalem, is also in the shape of a cube. The walls of the First Temple featured cedar wood engravings of gold-plated cherubim, palm trees, and blossoming flowers. The olivewood doorway into the inner chamber was engraved with the same golden images. Two olivewood cherubim, placed inside the Holy of Holies, had "wings that were stretched out so that the wing of the one touched the one wall, and the wing of the other touched the other wall" (1 Kings 6.27). King Solomon placed the Ark of the Covenant, which contained the tablets of stone, underneath the cherubim inside the inner chamber. The *kapporet* was positioned atop the ark as the throne, and G-d's presence appeared between the cherubim. Josephus described the Holy of Holies in the Second Temple as being covered in gold. The Temple's exterior walls and columns were made of white marble depicting the "whole vista of the heavens."

Josephus said, "But this Temple appeared to strangers as they approached, it seemed in the distance like a mountain covered with snow; for any part not covered with gold was dazzling white" (Josephus *The Wars of the Jews* 5.223).

Light was a key feature of the Temple. The *menorah* resembled "a tree of life, a tree of light, and a tree of fire." "It [was] through the *menorah* that the inner bond established through the incense offering was radiated throughout the world" (*The Incense Altar and the Menorah* Chabad.org). The kindling of the *menorah* was coupled with the daily incense offering in the Tabernacle. Every morning and evening, Aaron, the first high priest, burned fragrant incense on the golden altar before the curtain. He was commanded to burn the incense when he prepared the lamps of the menorah (Ex. 30.6-8).

In the midst of the garden sanctuary (Gen. 2.9) stood the Tree of Life: the *light* of the world. In John's Revelation vision, *Yeshua* says, "To him who overcomes I will give to eat from the Tree of Life, which is in the midst of the Paradise of G-d" (Rev 2.7). The *menorah*, or seven-branched lampstand, was the symbol of light in the Temple. In Revelation, John describes the *menorah* as being in the "midst of the garden." He says this knowing that the Second Temple *menorah* was located in the Holy Place — not in the Holy of Holies.

> And in the midst of the trees that of life, at that place where on the Lord rests, when he goes up into paradise; and this tree is of ineffable goodness and fragrance, and adorned more than every existing thing; and on all sides [it is] in form gold looking and vermillion and fire-like and covers all, and it has produce from all fruits. Its root is in the garden at the earth's end.
>
> (2 ENOCH 8.3,4)

Descriptions of the menorah (Ex. 25.31-40; 37.17-24) suggest it resembled a tree because its branches, leaves, petals, and almond-like blossoms extended from a central trunk. Philo thought the *menorah* was the Tree of Life in the garden and that the central shaft represented the king: an angelic being in the heavenly Tabernacle whose role was exemplified by the high priest in the earthly Temple. The seven lamps, symbolizing seven eyes, were mounted in such a way so as to give light to the space directly in front of the curtain leading into the Holy of Holies.

In the Ancient Near East a tree of life was a ritual symbol for both god and king (Widengren: 1951). The *menorah* was the symbol for the Divine Presence. Clement of Alexandria suggested *Yeshua* the Messiah was the *menorah* linked to the royal tree. Barker proposed that the lamp of the Temple represented the presence of G-d with His people and that it was the symbol of the dynasty. In the book of Revelation, the Son of Man stands among the seven lampstands. He is dressed as a *kohen* wearing the *ketonet* (a long-sleeved priestly robe) and a gold sash around his chest. As a link between John's revelation and Enoch's vision, Enoch saw a gold, fiery tree of great size in the garden. He identified it as the Tree of Life that originally stood in the garden sanctuary.

As for the likeness of the living creatures, their appearance was like burning coals of fire and like the appearance of lamps; it went up and down among the living creatures and the fire was bright and out of the fire went forth lightning. And the living creatures ran and returned as the appearance of a flash of lightning.

(EZEK. 1.13,14 RV)

This train of thought allows for another perspective of the burning bush. When the Angel of the Lord appeared to Moses at the Mountain of G-d, a blazing fire burned from inside a *sinai* (a thornbush). Although the bush was engulfed in flames, it was not consumed. This is likely a picture of the Tree of Life, the seven-branched *menorah*, with its bowls of anointing oil blazing in the midst of the garden sanctuary — holy ground to be sure. Interestingly, priests serving in the Temple precincts could not wear shoes.

> And the Angel of the Lord appeared to him in a flame of fire from the midst of a bush. So he looked, and behold, the bush was burning with fire, but the bush was not consumed. Then He said, "Do not draw near this place. Take your sandals off your feet, for the place where you stand is holy ground."
>
> (EX. 3.2,5)

Daniel's associates were thrown into a fiery furnace where they were not consumed by the fire. The furnace is likened to the Holy of Holies: the garden sanctuary where the *menorah* stood. *Avraham's* covenant with G-d, confirmed through a smoking furnace and burning torch passing between the halves of the animals, expressed similar imagery related to the incense and the menorah.

> And I beheld a vision, and lo, there was a second house, greater than the former and the entire portal stood open before me, and it was built of flames of fire. And its floor was of fire, and above it were lightnings and the path of the stars, and its ceiling also was flaming fire. And from underneath the throne came streams of flaming fire so that I could not look thereon. And the Great Glory sat thereon, and His raiment shone more brightly than the sun and was whiter than any snow. The flaming fire was round about Him and a great fire stood before Him and none around could draw nigh Him.
>
> (1 ENOCH 14.15-22)

So these men were tied up in their cloaks, tunics, robes and other clothes and thrown into the blazing hot furnace...didn't we throw three men, bound, into the flames? "Look!" he [Nebuchadnezzar] exclaimed, "I see four men loose, walking in the midſt of the fire; and they are not hurt, and the form of the fourth is like one of the gods." The viceroys, prefects, governors and royal advisers who were there saw that the fire had no power on the bodies of these men — not even their hair was singed, their clothes looked the same, and they didn't smell of fire.

(DAN. 3.21,24B-25,27)

Proverbs describes Wisdom as a tree of life, stating that, "whoever holds fast to *her* will be made honorable" (3.18). She was a tree whose fruit gave wisdom, whose leaves were for healing, and whose oil was used to open blind eyes. She represented the good fruit that comes from the restored Creation Covenant — described "sometimes as the Spirit and sometimes as righteousness" (Barker 2010: 250). A Targum to Genesis suggests the *Etz Chaim* (the Tree of Life) was the Torah linked to Wisdom. The Torah, written on the tablets of stone and containing the living words of G-d that He used to create the universe, were hidden away inside the ark: the oracle of G-d. *Yeshua* is the living Torah who came down from the heavenly sanctuary. He is the Tree of Life, the *menorah*: a symbol for both G-d and King. He is the anointed High Priest and Son of the Living G-d. Both the Bible and temple tradition describe the High Priest as the "anointed one" (Ex 30.30): the *Mashiach* (Messiah).

The sages often compared elements of the Temple to parts of the human body. This is a very complex subject that will be discussed in more detail in *The Temple Revealed in the Tents of the Patriarchs*. For now, I propose that the Temple was patterned after the head of a human being: the Holy Place being the face, the menorah the eyes, the table of showbread the mouth, the altar of incense the nose, and the Holy of Holies the skull with its two curtains representing either the double membrane of the skull or the two cranial hemispheres. According to this pattern, the Ark of the Covenant is the brain of the temple body.

In the center of the human brain, between the two hemispheres, is a small, pinecone-shaped gland called the pineal. The pineal gland regulates light in the body and controls a variety of functions including sleep patterns and the reproductive cycle. Pineal comes from the French word for pinecone and the Latin word for pine tree: *pinus*. Pine trees carry both male and female cones. In the ancient world, the cones were considered the source of life and a symbol of unity between male and female. ANE cultures saw pinecones as symbols of everlasting life, and they revered the pineal gland as the "god" organ. In these cultures, the pinecone pollinated their "tree of life." Ancient Assyrian palace carvings show a four-winged figure holding pinecones. Pinecones were symbols of the "mystic seed" that connected the physical and spiritual worlds. The pineal gland was the ancient symbol for human enlightenment and the spiritual center of the brain that opened eyes to see beyond physical reality. Called the third eye, the pineal is known as the storehouse of the imagination and is linked to the area of the brain that involves reasoning, intellect, and intuition.

The Hebrew word for pine is *oren*. The same Hebrew letters make up the word *aron*: ark. The pine tree was the *etz Shemen*: the oil tree in Second Temple writings related to the *menorah*. The same letters link the ark (*haAron*) to the high priest (*Aharon*). Aaron was the first high priest from the Levites to perform the *Yom Kippur* services of the blood and the incense before the ark in the Holy of Holies. *Aron* (ark) is also formed from two words: or and *nun*. *Or* means light and *nun* means seed (or fish in Aramaic). *Nun* is also a name for the Messiah who is called *Messiah Ben Nun*: son of fish/son of the continuing seed.

Learning to recognize the purpose and meaning of temple elements like the Holy of Holies, the ark, the high priest, the menorah, the cherubim, the animal offerings, and the service of the blood and the incense is key to understanding the atonement made by Messiah. The New Testament, in particular the book of Revelation, is filled with metaphors and allusions related to the *Yom Kippur* service. Without a working knowledge of temple language and imagery, many things don't make sense. This can lead to misinterpretation. In the last section of this chapter, we will look at a couple of familiar Scriptural examples where the Day of the Lord (*Yom Kippur*) imagery may well have been missed.

A Decidedly Different View

The New Testament/New Covenant is the Creation Covenant restored. This message of restoration is often communicated through parables: a method *Yeshua* used when teaching about the kingdom. Although many of his parables were stories well known to his audience, *Yeshua* always put a different spin on the punch line. This made the crowds sit up and take notice.

A parable is a proverb. From the Hebrew *mashal* (meaning rulership, dominion, or kingdom), parables/proverbs are part of the genre of wisdom literature and were the language of the Holy of Holies: the world behind the veil. Wisdom is symbolized by the *menorah*, the "Tree of Life (Prov. 3.18) to those who grasp her." For those who do, "they are made honorable in the kingdom."

Peter's vision of the sheet coming down from heaven (Acts 10.9-29) and the parable of the ten bridesmaids who took their oil lamps to meet the groom (Matt. 25.1-13) are both lessons about the Day of the Lord. A main theme in each example is the ministry of the high priest on *Yom Kippur*. Without knowledge of the Temple service, however, the parallels are easy to miss.

On *Yom Kippur*, the high priest immersed five times. Four

out of these five *tevillah* (immersions) took place on the roof of the *Parvah* chamber. This rooftop *mikvah* (immersion bath) was constructed exclusively for his use on that day. The roof of the *Parvah* chamber not only held the same level of sanctity as the inner courtyard of the Temple but was also designed specifically for the high priest's immersions. The meaning of *Parvah* is unknown, but it was likely connected to *parah*, cow, since the hides of the sacrificial animals were tanned and kept there for the priests. Because whoever stood on the roof was visible to those standing in the inner courtyard, the priests held up a white linen sheet made of a costly material. This allowed the high priest some privacy as he immersed in the *mikvah*, dried himself with the sheet, and dressed in his white linen garments. The linen sheet reminded him that he was performing the atonement service for *Yom Kippur* — clothed in white garments made of linen (Mishnah *Yoma* 3.4) reminiscent of the angels.

The key to deciphering Peter's vision is found in the purpose and meaning of the linen sheet. Peter received the vision during his stay at Simon the tanner's home in Jaffa. Simon's home was adjacent the Mediterranean Sea: a great place for immersions. Many have come to believe that the tanning process caused ritual impurity. According to Isaac Oliver, however, "Contact with dead bodies of kosher animals that were ritually slaughtered would not transmit ritual impurity." Additionally, the states that as long as the hides had no flesh attached to them (or flesh that was smaller than the size of an olive) no impurity was conveyed (BT *Chullin* 9.4). Therefore, there is no indication tanning ever caused any type of ritual defilement. Still, for hygienic reasons and because of its low socio-economic standing, tanning was genuinely frowned upon by the culture. The rabbis found the profession to be morally distasteful.

While Peter was praying on the roof of the tanner's house, he saw heaven open; the heavenly curtain was pulled back to reveal the Holy of Holies. The first connection to *Yom Kippur* is found here: before the high priest entered the Holy of Holies, he prayed, immersed, and changed his clothes on the roof of the Temple's tanning chamber. Then a voice told a hungry Peter to slaughter and eat. This is temple language that describes animal sacrifices which were food for the priests. Peter saw a large, white linen sheet lowered from heaven by its four corners. The priests held a linen sheet by its corners to give privacy to the high priest. On the sheet, Peter saw all kinds of unclean animals: four-footed animals, crawling creatures, and wild birds. The message being conveyed was neither a repudiation of the laws of ritual impurity nor approval for eating non-kosher foods. The message was that the Gentiles who believed in *Yeshua*, considered unclean because of their ritual impurity, had been made ritually pure. Wearing his resurrection clothing, the white linen garments of the high priest, *Yeshua* made atonement in the heavenly Holy of Holies. Peter's vision was not a value judgment on food; it was not an attempt to discredit the sacrifices in the Temple. It was the message of the Kingdom ensuring that *all* who received the atonement by faith would enter eternity wearing fine white garments.

In a similar vein, the parable of the ten virgins depicts the procession of the high priest to the Temple: a journey made seven days before *Yom Kippur*. On the morning of the journey, officials arrived at the high priest's home in Jerusalem in order to pray, instruct, and counsel him regarding the important day's services. As they prepared to leave for the Temple, a shout rang out calling the people to give honor to the high priest. The procession was accompanied by great fanfare and celebration. Those who lived in Jerusalem came out of their homes wearing white garments and carrying candles and burning torches. Every window was decorated with brightly lit lamps. A crier shouted for the people to give honor to the House of David and then to the House of Levi. Those with the highest status walked closest to the high priest. Descendants of Israel's kings began walking first. Close behind were the singers, musicians, and trumpeters. Next came those who prepared the incense and baked the bread; then walked the Temple guards and the Temple treasurers. The Sanhedrin then joined the procession followed by 250 priests. Each priest walked with his staff in his hand to clear a path for the high priest who was the last to walk. Many times the procession continued well past midnight, and most carried torches in order to light the way to the Temple. Once the high priest arrived at the Temple gate, he made his way to the *Palhedrin* chamber where he was sequestered for the next seven days. On the first day of his service, he went into the holy sanctuary to kindle five of the lamps in the seven-branched *menorah*. A little later he would prepare the last two.

The kingdom of heaven is like ten bridesmaids who took their lamps to meet the groom. In the march to the Temple gate, the high priest represented the bridegroom. Those who served in the Temple — the priests and Levites — were the bridesmaids. The Holy Temple itself was the bride, and the Holy of Holies was the bridal chamber/womb where the marriage would be consummated and new life produced. In *Yeshua's* telling of the parable, five bridesmaids carried no oil to serve the *menorah's* lamps while the other five came prepared with their flasks. When the bridegroom was late in arriving, the bridesmaids fell asleep. Suddenly, in the middle of the night, the crier shouted, "The bridegroom is here! Go out and meet him!" The five with oil were the prepared Temple servants who were ready to perform their services. The oil in their lamps represented Wisdom poured out in the form of the Spirit because of *Yeshua's* ministry in the heavenly Holy of Holies.

Hopefully these two examples make clear the importance of understanding temple imagery. This is especially true regarding the language of *Yom Kippur*: the Day of Atonement. The Bible refers to *Yom Kippur* as the "Day of the Lord" — an expression used by the patriarchs, the prophets, the mystics, and the New Testament writers. *The Day* is the final redemption, creation's restoration, and the fulfillment of *Yeshua's* atoning work.

✡ ✡ ✡

While writing this chapter, I had a dream in which I saw a large redbrick wall reaching to the sky. Slowly, an invisible hand began to remove each brick, one by one, until an elderly Jewish couple — dressed in the attire of the 1940s — stepped through the opening. The couple had apparently survived the persecution and devastation of WWII by hiding in this secret place. The woman carried a large manila folder full of handwritten documents. Without a word, she handed me the file that seemed to contain information detailing just how they had survived. As we sat together at the kitchen table, I peppered them with questions — asking about food and water storage, electricity, all things related to physical survival. The woman was the only one who spoke. Though her responses seemed vague and unhelpful, somehow I finally understood. The secret place, behind the bricks, was like the sanctuary in Moses's Song of the Sea. They had been hidden in the shelter of Almighty G-d in His Heavenly Sanctuary: the world outside of time. Chaos, death, and disorder had never found them. The documents were handwritten letters from the patriarchs and matriarchs explaining how they walked with G-d in times of trouble. Though I never actually read the documents, I instinctively knew that what they contained could be found in one other place: G-d's living Torah.

A special Siddur prayer included in the incense service is called *Ana Beko'ach*. It begins, "We beg you with the strength of your hand's greatness, untie the bundled sins." *Ana Beko'ach* is recited during the morning and evening prayer times. The entire prayer contains forty-two words to represent both the mystical name of G-d and the forty-two wilderness stations where Israel camped and His Divine Presence rested.

When G-d dwells in our midst, we will *know* true peace

regardless of the storms that rage around us. But He requires that we "hear" and "obey," that we seek Him in His Holy Sanctuary, and that we seek His Kingdom above all else. Therefore, with a heart full of gratitude and thanksgiving, set your affections on things above. The Day of the Lord, *Yom Kippur*, is coming! On that day, *Yeshua* will judge the nations. Once and for all, we will finally be set free from the burden of sin and death.

CHAPTER FIVE

G-D AND HIS BRIDE

Happy (ashrei) is the person who finds wisdom,
the person who acquires understanding. She is a tree
of life to those who grasp her; whoever holds fast to her
will be made happy (ashrei).
(Prov. 3.13,18)

No family is complete without the real "power behind the throne": the wife and mother of the house. She is the heart and soul of the family and the operations manager who oversees the orderly functioning of the home. Her responsibilities are endless! She is the Proverbs 31 woman — achieving success both at home and in business while ensuring that her household is charitable. She is the teacher, nurturer, comforter, and protector who provides for her family's emotional stability. She creates an environment of love and spiritual harmony to embolden each member's personal growth. She is ever the optimist — confident, wise, and kind. She is celebrated both for her practical and spiritual strength. She is unceasing in bolstering her husband's role as a leader in the community. She is the *Eishet Chayil*, the Woman of Valor, whose light never goes out. "Her mouth opens with wisdom, and loving instruction is on her tongue" (Prov. 31.26). Her virtues build her house; she is a woman who fears the Lord.

Proverbs 31 is an allegory about a woman named Wisdom. She was the noble wife of the king. In a literal sense, it was written as a tribute to Bathsheba: wife of King David and mother of King Solomon. On a deeper, allegorical level, the Woman of Valor *personifies* the Spirit of Wisdom. It is "Wisdom who built herself a house" (Prov. 9.1). Philo referred to G-d as the husband of Wisdom (*On the Cherbim* 43-44) and declared, "G-d is both a house, the incorporeal abode... the husband of wisdom, sowing for the race of mankind the seed of happiness in good and virgin soil" (49). "Adam came into being through two virgins — through the spirit and through the virgin earth" (Gospel of Philip 74). First-century extra-biblical literature shows Wisdom and the Holy Spirit to be one and the same (Wisdom of Solomon 9.17).

In the book of Proverbs, Wisdom is revealed as co-creator with her husband, G-d. "G-d by Wisdom founded the earth, by understanding, He established the heavens" (Prov. 3:19).

Adonai made me [wisdom] as the beginning of his way, the first of his ancient works. I was appointed before the world, before the start, before the earth's beginnings. When I was brought forth, there were no ocean depths, no springs brimming with water. I was brought forth before the hills, before the mountains had settled in place; he had not yet made the earth, the fields, or even the earth's first grains of dust. When he established the heavens, I was there. When he drew the horizon's circle on the deep, when he set the skies above in place, when the foundations of the deep poured forth, when he prescribed boundaries for the sea...when he marked out the foundations of the earth, I was with him as someone he could trust.

(PROV. 8.22-30)

Her [wisdom], I [Solomon] loved and sought out from my youth, and I sought to take her for my bride...she proclaimed her noble birth in that it is given her to live with G-d, and the Sovereign Lord of all loved her. For she is initiated into the knowledge of G-d and she chose out [for him] his works. The fruits of wisdom's labor are virtues for she teaches self-control and understanding, righteousness and courage. She knows the things of old and divines the things to come. She foresees signs and wonders, and the issues of seasons and times. I determined therefore to take her unto me to live with me knowing that she is one who would give me good [thoughts] of counsel and encourage me in cares and grief.

(WISDOM OF SOLOMON 8.1-4,7-9)

Wisdom was "understanding" who raised her voice and spoke words that were righteous and true; she was better than pearls, and she was appointed before the world — before earth's beginnings. She was there when G-d established the heavens, and she built herself a house carved with seven pillars. She was the life-giving force, the power of G-d, the agent of creation, and the mother of all. For the "House of Jacob signifies the mother of creation" and "thanks to the mother the world itself is sustained and all creation becomes a dwelling place; thanks to the mother, creation has meaning."

(PATTERSON 2005: 23)

Rashi said it was through the mother that the Torah, the Wisdom of the universe, was given. "Bearing life into the world, she bears the Torah into the world." *Midrash Proverbs* (an early commentary ca. 9th century CE) states that "Wisdom" alludes to the Torah.

The Book of Proverbs, *Mishlei* in Hebrew, is part of the genre of wisdom literature. The Aramaic Targum calls Wisdom a "skilled woman" with talents related to house/ temple building activities. In the verse, "She considers a field and buys it, and from her earnings she plants a vineyard," is found figurative, temple-building language (Prov. 31.16). "She is clothed in fine linen and purple" brings to mind the woven garments of the high priest and invokes images of the curtain in front of the Holy of Holies. The Temple described in Revelation (17.4) is called "the harlot" — corrupted by the priestly leadership. Like the high priest, the harlot is "dressed in purple and scarlet" — glittering with gold, precious stones, and pearls. Throughout the Book of Proverbs, the noble and wise wife is contrasted with the foolish harlot.

Some attribute the Woman of Valor allegory to Sarah, wife of *Avraham*, while others suggest this honored woman is representative of all the Old Testament women — the matriarchs in particular. The matriarchs were ultimately responsible for building the greatest house of all: Israel.

> The innocent and un-begotten Adam, being the type and resemblance of G-d the Father Almighty...His begotten son [Seth] shadowing forth the image of the begotten Son and word of G-d; while Eve signifies the person and procession of the Holy Spirit.
>
> (QUOTED IN BARKER, ANTI-NICENE FATHERS VOL. 6: 402)

> The *Shekinah* in the time of Abraham our father is called Sarah, and in the time of Isaac our father is called Rebecca, and in the time of Jacob our father is called Rachel.
>
> (GIKATILLA 1994: 204)

Each Friday night in Jewish homes, the husband recites *Eishet Chayil* (Prov. 31, the Woman of Valor) over his wife. She sits at the table as a queen while those around sing her praises. Scholars say this custom dates back to the Kabbalists of the seventeenth century who saw the *Shabbat* (Sabbath) as a time for the "mystical union" between G-d and His Queen. This Queen is the *Shekinah*, the divine presence, to whom Proverb's Woman of Valor is also attributed.

The Talmudic sages envisaged the *Shekinah* as a spiritual essence of indescribable beauty. Perhaps this is why the matriarchs are also described as being especially beautiful. In the *Tanakh* (OT), women's names often describe the workings of the Holy Spirit. *Sarah* is the princess, *Rebecca* is a yoke that ties two together, and *Rachel* is the prescribed path of learning. *Zipporah* (wife of Moses) is the heavenly bird, *Yochebed* (mother of Moses) is the glory of Yah, and *Miriam* (sister of Moses) is the myrrh of the anointing oil. Of Moses's midwives, *Puah* is the soothing, calm voice, and *Shaphar* is the one who beautifies newborn babies. *BatSheva* (Bathsheba) is the daughter of seven for the sevenfold Spirit, *Elisheva* (Elizabeth) is "my G-d is seven," *Malkat Sheva* (the Queen of Sheba) is the Queen of Seven, and *Deborah* is the *Debir*: the Holy of Holies. Together, these women present a powerful portrait of the co-creator of the House of G-d: the Holy Spirit.

In the ANE, the god and his consort took up residence in their newly constructed temple. Their sacred wedding was a seven-day temple dedication, and the couple's union guaranteed the fertility of the land and the fruitfulness of the people. The Holy of Holies, the world outside of time, is the inner sanctum of the cosmic Temple where G-d resides with Wisdom, His Bride. Together, G-d and Wisdom created the world. According to the Gospel of Philip, the Holy of Holies is the bridal chamber where the son was born. It is the place of divine light, and a great fire appeared at the son's birth:

The Father of everything united with the virgin who came down and a fire shone for him on that day. He appeared in the great bridal chamber. Therefore his body came into being on that very Day. It left the bridal chamber as one who came into being from the bridegroom and the bride… the mysteries of this marriage are perfected rather in the day and in the light. Neither that day nor its light ever sets. If anyone becomes a son of the bridal chamber, he will receive the light.

(GOSPEL OF PHILIP 71)

From the joys of marriage and birth to the sorrows of death and loss, the stories surrounding the Old Testament families illustrate the plight of every family. Alongside their dysfunction, and fractious interpersonal relationships, came great successes and blessing through their progeny. Their stories mirror life in the practical realm and hint at something deeper in the spiritual realm. The deeper understanding is what defines a parable/proverb: a story or riddle with two meanings — one plain and the other hidden.

Yeshua taught in parables. He shared the common understanding with the people but explained the hidden meaning to his disciples: "To you has been given to know secrets of the kingdom" (Matt 13.11). "Listen my people to my teaching, turn your ears to the words from my mouth. I will speak to you in parables and explain mysteries from days of old" (Ps. 78.2).

The beatitudes (Matt 5.3-10) are parables, teachings, about the kingdom and the world beyond time. In Hebrew, beatitude is *ashrei* and translates "happy is," "praiseworthy is," "oh the joy of," or "honorable is." The message of *ashrei* is that honor and joy come to those who dwell in G-d's house and follow His instructions. Psalm 145 is called *the Ashrei,* and the Talmud (*Berachot* 4b) states that those who recite it three times a day are assured a place in The World to Come.

Ashrei are those who dwell in your house; may they always praise you, Selah! *Ashrei* is the people for whom this is so, *ashrei* is the people whose G-d is the Lord.

(BENEDICTION FOR PSALM 145)

The root of *ashrei* is *asher* which means "straight." Therefore, one who is happy lives a straight life on the straight and narrow path. *Ashrei* is always connected to the Temple and the kingdom. "*Ashrei* are those whose way is perfect, who walk with the Torah of G-d" (Ps. 119.1). "*Ashrei* are those who do His commandments, that they may have the right to the Tree of Life, and may enter through the gates into the city" (Rev. 22.14 NKJV). Proverbs and parables are instructions for the proper functioning of the house. This knowledge brings the joy of fruitful living and represents the work and ministry of the Holy Spirit.

Asherah and the Ancients

Asherah also comes from the root *asher*. The goddess Asherah had a very storied history; she morphed into multiple forms and was given a variety of names in the cultures of the ANE. When the ancient Hebrews settled in the land of Canaan, they embraced this fertility goddess as part of their cultic practices. A tree trunk was thought to be a *Beth-El*: a "house of the deity." So Asherah was represented by a wooden pole or tree that was planted in the ground on a hilltop or under a leafy tree (Patai 1990: 45). With branches extended, she looked like the Tree of Life which was a common image in the ANE and a symbol for Wisdom going back to the garden sanctuary. In the Assyrian culture, for example, she was called *Asirtu*: "sanctuary." To the Hebrew people, a man's wife was called his house. They saw the *mikdash*, the holy sanctuary, as a representation of G-d's spouse.

Jewish scholar Raphael Patai explained that reconstruction of the earlier Hebrew religion is based on four things: the evidence in the Bible (which contains incidental information regarding popular religion), local archaeological evidence (mostly limited but useful), detailed information about the deities they worshipped based on the archaeology and mythology of ancient Canaan, Syria, and Mesopotamia etc., and literary sources from the first centuries of the Christian era. He noted an absence of literary documents — that is, inscriptions on tablets, monuments, and statues — that usually provide evidence for cult worship. The limited available evidence does suggest, though, that the ancient Hebrew people were unduly influenced by the Canaanites' pantheon of gods and goddesses — in particular the goddess Asherah. In the nearly six centuries between the time they settled in Canaan and the Babylonian exile, the Israelites worshipped her alongside their worship of Yahweh. "There are inscriptions as old as 800 BCE that contain blessings by Yahweh and his consort, Asherah. It appears they were a very popular couple worshipped for centuries prior to the religious changes introduced by King Josiah"(Patai 1990: 35-40).

Based on material found at Ras Shamra (the ancient Phoenician city of Ugarit in the NW corner of Syria on the Mediterranean), Asherah became the chief goddess of the Canaanite pantheon around the fourteenth century BCE. She was the wife of El, their chief god, and she ruled beside him as queen. She was known as "Lady Asherah of the Sea" or "She Who Treads on the Sea," for the sea was her domain. She was the mother goddess who served as wet-nurse for the gods and kings who were said to receive the divine right to rule through her milk. She was represented by carved wooden images planted in the ground next to altars dedicated to Ba'al. Archaeologists have found an abundance of female figurines (no male ones) that indicate her worship was very popular — likely because she promoted fertility and helped in childbirth (36-41).

Asherah worship remained popular among the tribes of Israel for the next three centuries — well into the reign of Solomon who also worshipped her as the Goddess of the Sidonians (1 Kings 11.5). Nearly all the kings of Judah and Israel worshipped Asherah. Solomon's son, Rehoboam, married Abshalom's daughter, Maachah. Maachah brought the image of the goddess into the Jerusalem Temple. In response, King Asa removed Maachah as queen mother; he cut down the image and burned it by the Brook Kidron (1 Kings 15.13). Likewise, King Hezekiah repaired, restored, and reformed the Temple after the devastation brought by his father, Ahaz. Hezekiah removed the unauthorized high places that were in service when the Temple was standing (many high places were legitimate sites when there was no temple), smashed the standing stones, and cut down the Asherah (2 Kings 18.4). This purity would not last, however; Hezekiah's son, King Manasseh, erected the carved image once again (2 Kings 21.3). Patai asked: "Was Manasseh's act the conviction that Yahweh's consort, the great mother-goddess Asherah, must be restored to her old and lawful place at the side of her husband?"

When King Josiah found the scroll of the Torah (Deuteronomy), he made a covenant in the presence of G-d to follow His commandments wholeheartedly. In an attempt to restore the Temple, the services, and the people back to G-d, Josiah instituted the greatest reforms of all which included the removal of Asherah:

And the king [Josiah] commanded Hilkiah, the high priest, the priests of the second order, and the doorkeepers, to bring out of the Temple of the Lord all the articles that were made for Baal, for Asherah, and for all the host of heaven; and he burned them outside Jerusalem in the fields of Kidron, and carried their ashes to Bethel...And he brought out the wooden image [Asherah] from the house of the Lord, to the Brook Kidron outside Jerusalem, burned it at the Brook Kidron and ground it to ashes, and threw its ashes on the graves of the common people.

King Josiah, considered the greatest Yahwist (early source from the Torah) reformer of all (621 BCE), instituted purges to cleanse the Temple and restore Israel's worship to G-d alone. The Deuteronomists (a movement whose material is based on Deuteronomy), as they came to be known, would not tolerate the worship of any but Yahweh. These reforms created a gulf between them and those of the earlier religion who continued to worship the goddess.

After King Josiah died, Asherah returned to the Temple where she remained until its destruction by the Babylonians under King Nebuchadnezzar (586 BCE). All in all, the image of Asherah was included in Temple worship more than it was not. Her worship played a significant role in ancient Israel's religion. Asherah, the motherly figure, must have been "dear to many worshippers and her restoration to the traditional place in the Temple was therefore considered a religious act of great importance" (Patai 1990: 49).

Both King Josiah and the prophet Jeremiah attempted to purge Israel of its worship of Yahweh's "queen." By the end of the seventh century BCE, Jeremiah observed that in times of distress the Israelite women would "bake ritual cakes for the Queen of heaven." The people poured out their libations and burned incense to her because they believed she had the power to avert disaster. Jeremiah, who prophesied between Josiah's death (609 BCE) and the Babylonian exile (586 BCE), railed against the altars of Asherah that were "under every leafy tree" and "upon every high hill" in Israel (Jer. 17.2). The Israelites refused to listen to Jeremiah's warnings:

> But we will certainly do whatever has gone out of our own mouth, to burn incense to the queen of heaven and pour out drink offerings to her, as we have done, we and our

fathers, our kings and our princes, in the cities of Judah and in the streets of Jerusalem. For then we had plenty of food, were well off, and saw no trouble. But since we stopped offering to the queen of heaven and pouring out drink offerings to her, we have lacked everything, and we have been destroyed by sword and famine. The wives added, are we the ones who offer to the queen of heaven? Do we pour out drink offerings to her? And did we make cakes marked with her image for her and pour out drink offerings to her without our husbands' consent?

(JER. 44.17-19 NKJV)

Jeremiah explained the reasons for the disaster that had befallen them. He said it was because of their detestable deeds: they offered incense to the queen, they sinned against G-d, they hardened themselves to the warnings He sent them, and they refused to live by His Torah. G-d responded:

You and your wives have spoken with your mouths and fulfilled with your hands, saying, "We will surely keep our vows that we have made, to burn incense to the queen of heaven and pour out drink offerings to her." You will surely keep your vows and perform your vows!

(JER. 44.25 NKJV)

The consequence for their disobedience, according to the Deuteronomists, was the destruction of the First Temple and exile to Babylon. The prophet Ezekiel detailed the idolatrous practices taking place in the Jerusalem Temple. He described the "image of jealousy" that stood near the northern gate leading to the altar. Biblical scholars have suggested this was the image of Asherah originally set up by King Manasseh. "In the eyes of the Yahwists, to whom belonged a few of the kings and all of the prophets, the worship of Asherah was an abomination. It had to be because it was a cult accepted by the Hebrews from their Canaanite neighbors" (Patai 1990: 52).

The unanswered question is exactly what hold Asherah, the mother goddess, had over the ancient people. Patai pondered whether the goddess was more of a complementary figure rather than one existing in competition with Yahweh. "One cannot belittle the emotional gratification with which she must have rewarded her servants who saw in her the loving motherly consort of the Yahweh-Baal and for whom she was the great mother-goddess, giver of fertility, that greatest of all blessings. The Hebrew people by and large clung to her for six centuries" (52).

In his article, "Did Yahweh Have a Consort?" (1979: 24-34), Ze'ev Meshel described some unique inscriptions he discovered on two large storage jars found in Kuntillet Ajrud: a remote desert way station in the wilderness of the northern Sinai. The inscriptions, along with some religious drawings, were left behind by traders in the early eighth century BCE. Although the site was not a temple complex, it *was* a religious center. The storage jars, each over three feet high, feature preserved inscriptions related to the worship of Asherah. One inscription reads, "I have blessed you by Yahweh *shmrn* (guard or the city of *Shomron*) and his *srth* (Asherah)." The last word, *srth*, is in the possessive form: *Asherato*. This could mean "His *cella*" or "His holy of holies." It could also mean "His tree" (a symbol of the deity) or "His consort." Meshel suggested that two of the three figures found on the jars may have also represented Yahweh and his consort. On an artifact found nine miles west of Hebron, another inscription reads, "Uriah the rich has caused it to be written: Blessed be Uriah by Yahweh and by his Asherah; from his enemies he has saved him." These "inscriptions show that in the popular religion of the time, the Goddess Asherah was associated with Yahweh, probably his wife, and that Yahweh and his Asherah were the most popular divine couple" (Patai 1990: 53).

In Kuntillet Ajrud, Meshel also found a large quantity

of finely woven linen. This caused him to hypothesize that a group of priests may have lived there. The fabric was made from quality yarn that was evenly woven. In fact, the "pieces of cloth were woven together so neatly and carefully and with such a fine needle that it resembled today's invisible mending." Patai noted that no one is really sure how the ancient Hebrews served Asherah except for one obscure detail: the women were weaving "houses" for her in the Jerusalem Temple (52).

> He [Josiah] smashed the houses of the cult prostitutes that were in the house of *Adonai* where the women also wove garments for the Asherah.
>
> (2 KINGS 23.7)

Young, virgin women were responsible for large amounts of weaving in the Temple. In particular, they were the weavers of the *parokhet* (curtain) and the priestly garments (BT *Tamid* 29b). According to the Infancy Gospel of James written around 145 CE (1.10-11), Mary, mother of *Yeshua*, was among the young women chosen to make the veils for the Temple. Legend has it that while she was weaving the angel Gabriel appeared bringing good news of the birth of the Messiah. Mary, one of seven virgins chosen from the family of David, was responsible for spinning the scarlet and purple threads. Composed shortly after the destruction of the Temple in 70 CE, *Baruch* made reference to "virgins; who weave fine linen and silk with the gold of Ophir" (Apocalypse of Baruch 10.19). Rashi, in his commentary on First Chronicles (20.5), declared that King David's mother was also engaged in weaving the Temple *parokhet*.

In his article, "Cosmos, Temple, House: Building and Wisdom in Ancient Mesopotamia and Israel," Raymond Van Leeuwen said, "All the wise hearted women who weave cloth for the Tabernacle 'with wisdom' have their counterpart in the valiant woman of Proverbs 31. She manufactures for her house the same types of fine cloth in G-d's house" (Ed.

Clifford 2007: 417). The walls of the Tabernacle were also constructed from cloth woven by women. In the ANE, textile work was a metaphor for women's wisdom. This reinforces the notion that the ancient Israelite women built their houses with the attribute of wisdom.

As an interesting aside, "The Women of the Veil Chamber," a small group of women living in the biblical Samarian community of Shiloh, are recreating the *parokhet*: the curtain that separated the Holy Place from the Holy of Holies. They say learning how to weave the veil is a way of preparing for the rebuilding of the Temple.

> You shall make a veil woven of blue, purple, and scarlet thread, and fine woven line. It shall be woven with an artistic design of cherubim.
>
> (EX. 26.31)

A Feminine Holy Spirit

> She [Wisdom] proclaimed her noble birth in that it is given her to live with G-d, and the Sovereign Lord of all loved her. When I come into my house, I shall find rest with her; for converse with her has not bitterness. And to live with her has not pain, but gladness and joy.
>
> [WISDOM OF SOLOMON 8.3,16]

When the First Temple was destroyed, the priests explained that the nation was being judged by G-d for their devotion to Asherah. Seen as an idolatrous and adulterous act, the worship of the Queen of Heaven brought judgment from an angry and jealous G-d. On the other hand, some scholars have suggested the priests had simply shifted the blame for their leadership failures to frame the disaster in more theological terms (DeConick 2011: 14). Overall, the priests were successful in suppressing the worship of the goddess. In the eyes of the older religious cult, however, when the people of Israel rejected Wisdom (the motherly Spirit figure) they were sent into exile away from their central sanctuary where Wisdom once dwelled.

By the end of the exilic period, the Deuteronomists had replaced Asherah as Yahweh's wife with the nation of Israel. However, "she is not forgotten, her story echoes in the written memories that make up the Jewish wisdom literature, memories of a co-creator angel, a female spirit who comes to earth to rest in the prophets and redeem the people of Israel" (14). In the New Testament, "She is even able to regain most of her former glory...when she re-emerges in the early Christian tradition as the Holy Spirit" (15). In the Semitic languages, the "Spirit" is grammatically feminine. Many of the extra-biblical writings of the Second Temple period also convey a Holy Spirit that is feminine.

Ruach HaKodesh (Holy Spirit) is a feminine noun in both Hebrew and Aramaic (*ruha*). To the first Christians, who were Jews, the Spirit was undeniably feminine. They likely understood that when G-d created man in "our image," the Bible was referring to G-d, the Father, and the Holy Spirit, the mother. "Both genders were created simultaneously to reflect the image of the male and female *Elohim*" (8). When the Bible instructs, "a man shall leave his father and mother," they understood that Adam's father was G-d and his mother was G-d's consort, Wisdom/the Holy Spirit.

There are a few familiar word pairs that highlight the relationship between G-d and His queen. *Eishet* (f.) *Chayil* (m.) is the Woman of Valor or strength. *Ruach* (f.) *Elohim* (m.) is the Spirit of G-d hovering over the waters. *Malkut* (f.) *Shemayim* (m.) is the Kingdom of Heaven that is near. A home is always referred to as *malchut*: a feminine noun for kingdom. For this reason, a man's home is also called his wife.

By the close of the second century, the Holy Spirit was no

longer widely viewed as a feminine entity. In Greek, *pneuma* (spirit) is grammatically neutral. In other languages, such as Latin, "Holy Spirit" is masculine. By the fourth century CE, the Holy Spirit was largely seen as a shapeless male entity sent from the Father to inspire the church. But for the Gnostics of the time, she remained the feminine Holy Spirit. They explained the G-dhead as a trinity: the Father, the Mother, and the Son (DeConick 2011). In the Jewish tradition, the Holy Spirit was an independent angel who existed before creation and was co-creator with G-d. She was enthroned next to her husband in clouds of heaven. Clement of Alexandria (early third century) said, "she (Holy Spirit) is an indwelling bride."

In the fourth century, the exaltation of the Virgin Mary exploded. She was given titles once associated with Asherah: Virgin, Bride, Mother of G-d, and Queen of Heaven. In the age of the Talmud (up to the seventh century), the feminine Spirit emerged as the *Shekinah*: G-d's Divine presence. By the tenth century CE, the Jewish mystical tradition known as Kabbalah (receiving) had cemented the *Shekinah* as the feminine manifestation of G-d. For the Kabbalists, the union between G-d, the king and the Shekinah, His queen provided protection for Israel on the Sabbath. In their minds, the behavior of Israel determined the relationship between the divine couple. Sin kept them apart and gave power to the forces of evil. Repentance and piety brought them together in a love affair that restored their unity. It was said the coming of the Messiah would enable a permanent reunification of the divine lovers (Patai 1990: 155).

Ancient Israel's view of the genuine Queen of Heaven, the Holy Spirit, survived in the earliest Aramaic Christian literature — from the imagery of a mother bird and the Spirit of G-d hovering (feminine verb) over the waters to the Tree of Life as Wisdom and feminine co-creator. In time, grammatical rules no longer mattered, and the Aramaic *ruha* became masculine — *only* when referring to the Holy Spirit. In the sixth century, traces of a feminine Holy Spirit still survived in some of the liturgical writings and poetry. These were mainly connected to water immersion and Eucharistic rituals related to the Mother Spirit hovering over the waters (DeConick 2011).

Examples of a feminine Holy Spirit were plentiful in the early Syriac church. Ephrem, a theologian and father of the Syrian church in the fourth century CE, referred to the Holy Spirit as the mother. When the dove descended on *Yeshua* at his immersion, Ephrem said, "The Spirit descended from on high and she sanctified the water by her hovering. The Holy Spirit is feminine and is the mother of Jesus. She calls out to him at baptism, 'This is my beloved Son'..."(*Epiphany Hymn* 6.1). In the Syrian tradition, the baptismal waters were depicted as a womb from which we are reborn, and the Spirit is the mother who gives birth to us (DeConick 2011: 25).

Aphraates, a Persian Jew who converted to Christianity, declared, "From baptism we receive the Spirit of Christ and in the same hour that the priests invoke the Spirit, she opens the heavens and descends and hovers over the waters, and those who are baptized put her on. From all who are born of a body, the Spirit is absent until they come to birth by water and then receive the Holy Spirit" (*Demonstrations* 6.292.24-293.5). He also taught that the wording, "a man shall leave his father and his mother," (Gen. 2.24) does not refer to ordinary parents but to the heavenly Father and the Mother Spirit. "Who leaves father and mother to take a wife? The meaning is as follows: as long as a man has not taken a wife, he loves and reveres G-d his father and the Holy Spirit his mother, and he has no other love. But when a man takes a wife, then he leaves his (true) father and his mother" (*Demonstrations* 18).

Macarious, a fourth century monk from NE Syria, said, "Once the 'veil of darkness' came upon Adam's soul, humans have been unable to see the true heavenly father and the good kind Mother, the grace of the Spirit and the sweet and desired Brother, the Lord" (DeConick, 2011: 22).

The Gospel of Thomas is an early third-century Christian text also from eastern Syria. When referencing the immersion of a number of young men, it says, "Come gift to the Most High! Come compassionate Mother! Come partner of the male! Come revealer of secret mysteries! Take part with these young men! Come Holy Spirit and cleanse their loins and their hearts. And seal them in the name of the Father and the Son and the Holy Spirit." In the Gospel of Thomas, part of the *Nag Hammadi Texts* (discovered 1945-47), *Yeshua* refers to himself as the Son of the Holy Spirit. He declares that his disciples must hate their earthly parents but love the Father and the Mother as he does: "For my mother gave me falsehood but my true mother gave me life." In time, Syriac copies of this gospel completely erased all references to the mother Spirit.

In 600 CE, the bishop Martyrius (of Mahoze) depicted the Christian convert as one "who has been held worthy of the hovering of the all-holy Spirit, who, like a mother hovers over us as she gives sanctification and through her hovering over us, we are made worthy of sonship."

The Odes of Solomon (written in Greek) were likely recorded first in Aramaic or Syrian around 100-125 CE. (Scholars originally thought they were Jewish writings.) Contained in the forty-two hymns are a few references to the feminine Holy Spirit. Many of these odes were recited during immersion ceremonies. For instance, the joy of the "Mother Spirit" when she declared Jesus her son is recorded: "the dove fluttered over the head of our Lord messiah because he was her head. And she cooed over him, and her voice was heard" (Ode 24). "I rested on the Spirit of the Lord and she raised me up to heaven and caused me to stand on my feet in the Lord's high place" (Ode 36).

The Gospel of Hebrews was referenced by both Jerome and Origen and was regarded by some as the original record of *Yeshua's* life. Although the Greek version was quite popular in Alexandria, Egypt during the second century CE, it is at least as old as the Gospels in the *New Testament*. This gospel remains the subject of much debate. However, it does portray the feminine Holy Spirit descending on Jesus at his immersion: "My son in all the prophets was I waiting for you that you should come and I might rest in you, for you are my rest. You are my firstborn Son who reigns forever." Instead of being taken to the wilderness to be tempted by Satan, this gospel states Jesus was taken by the Spirit to the top of Mount Tabor. *Yeshua* said, "My mother the Holy Spirit took me by one of the hairs on my head and bore me off to the great mountain Tabor" (Quoted by Origen, Commentary on John 2.12.87). The early Christians assumed that when the son was immersed and raised up out of the water, and when the Spirit rested upon him, he became the divine king. To them, his immersion was an ancient coronation ritual (Codex Bezea on Luke 3.22) confirmed when the heavenly voice declared, "You are my son; today I have begotten you" (Ps. 2.7b). To become king was to be "born again" (in water) to heavenly parents after being born the first time to earthly parents. "Son of G-d" was the title given to the Davidic kings descended from G-d's adopted son, Solomon.

> As soon as *Yeshua* had been immersed, he came up out of the water. At that moment heaven opened, he saw the Spirit of G-d coming down upon him like a dove, and a voice from heaven said, This is my Son, whom I love; I am well pleased with him.
>
> (MATT. 3.16,17)

In connection to his water immersion, most of the early Christian sources refer to the Holy Spirit as the mother of *Yeshua*. They tie the Spirit descending upon him like a dove to the Spirit of G-d hovering over the face of the waters (Gen. 1.2). This is the image of a mother bird hovering over her nest: an idiom in the Jewish tradition for the *Shekinah* (indwelling presence). The voice speaking from heaven at his immersion was *Yeshua's* mother, Wisdom, or what we call the Holy Spirit today.

Wisdom is a Queen

Send her forth out of the holy heavens and from the throne of your glory...so that she may toil with me. For she knows all things and has understanding thereof...she shall guard me in her glory that I may learn what is well pleasing before you. She will help me judge your people righteously and I shall be worthy of my father's throne.

(WISDOM OF SOLOMON 9.10-12)

If we were to picture the Holy Spirit from the record of early Christian belief, we might glimpse this feminine person of Wisdom as a queen in the heavenly royal court. We might find her seated beside G-d on her own throne in heaven but one with Him, and submissive to Him, as a wife is to her husband. In my research for this book, I was struck by a correlation between the person of Wisdom and Scripture's mysterious Queen of Sheba (I Kings 10.1-10). We are accustomed to male figures making their appearances on earth, but what form would the Holy Spirit take when visiting the earthly realm? The following fictional vignette connects the Queen of Sheba (Queen of Seven) to the person of Wisdom:

When she heard the news, *Malkat Sheva*, the Queen of Seven, opened her eyes and sat upright on her bejeweled sapphire throne. For confirmation concerning this glorious report, she looked to her King who was seated beside her on the royal throne. Together, the Queen and *HaMelech* (the King) ruled the universe from their lofty perch in the seventh heaven, the *Aravot*, where the dew was stored up for the righteous in the World to Come. Seven blazing torches encircled their thrones, and from underneath poured forth streams of flaming fire. A sweet aroma emanated from the succulent fruit of the Tree of Life; it permeated the heavenly air. Monstrous-sized golden cherubim, their wings outstretched, brandishing swords, cast giant shadows overhead. The glass ceiling displayed the path of the great luminaries — including the treasuries of the stars. In front of the thrones, a brightly illuminated sapphire floor projected a deep blue hue onto the firmament below: the cornerstone of the kingdom. From it rose a mountain-sized Rock filled with fine gems and precious stones. Marked with the footsteps of the angels, a path of luminescent pearls and fiery red rubies led into the throne room. Twenty-four enthroned elders of the royal angelic priesthood sat dressed in dazzling white robes with golden crowns upon their heads. They paid homage to the great ruler with shouts of "Blessed, praised, glorified, exalted is the holy King with all greatness, strength, splendor, triumph, glory, power and majesty!" The heavenly host offered up fragrant spices of myrrh and frankincense, along with prayers, just as their priestly counterparts did below.

Solomon, King of Israel, had been commissioned to build a royal temple, and the work was now complete. Shouts of joy rang throughout the throne room. G-d's earthly House had been readied for the King. The House was covered in white marble stone that resembled the garments the high priest wore on the Day of Atonement. Dedication day had arrived, and the altar was ready for thousands of oxen and sheep to be offered; the sweet savor from the burnt offerings would reach the heavenly throne room. This glorious gathering on earth would be celebrated for two sets of seven days.

During the dedication, the Temple's craftsmen would be honored for their fine, meticulous, bronze work. Hiram, of the tribe of Naftali, had been filled with wisdom, understanding, and the skill necessary to build a glorious house for the King. He had been transported to the heavenly realms and shown the original blueprints of creation. He received the list of materials, the measurements, and the designs for all the vessels and furniture. King Solomon then sought out merchants the world over in order to purchase what was needed. Just like Bezalel, the master craftsman of the Tabernacle before him, Hiram made everything according to what *HaMelech* had ordered. Solomon's Temple perfectly reflected the very essence of the world beyond the firmament.

When the chariot throne was placed inside the Holy of Holies, Solomon declared, "I have built you a magnificent house — a place where you can live forever." He then made his way outside to the brazen altar of burnt offering. In the presence of the entire community, he spread out his hands toward heaven and cried out, "G-d of Israel, there is no G-d like you in heaven above or on earth below." Great applause and cheers of "Long Live the King!" rose from the Temple to the heavenly court. Order and stability had come to the earth.

It was agreed *Malkat Sheva*, the Queen of Seven, would descend from her heavenly throne to meet with King Solomon and witness the dedication of the newly completed Temple. Her chariot was prepared — its wheels oiled with holy oil. Her purpose in descending was to lift Solomon as a banner over the whole earth. Before she arrived, *Malkat Sheva* sent ships loaded with costly gifts to fill the Temple. She made ready her sizeable retinue that included thousands of young men dressed in purple garments finely woven by the angels in heaven. The gateway to the southern heavens split open as *Malkat Sheva*, riding her golden chariot, passed through the firmament's portal. Once she reached the land of Israel, she traveled on camels bearing spices such as frankincense and myrrh, gold from Ophir, and precious stones mined from the Rock inside the heavenly Holy of Holies. The south wind approached the chariot for the final leg of her journey to the secret place in the Negev, near the *Aravah* (willow), that was once the watering hole for *Avraham's* sheep. She joined the caravansary as they made their way up to Jerusalem.

King Solomon was told of a queen of high rank who was

on her way to his kingdom, and he was intrigued. He had surpassed the kings of the earth in both wealth and wisdom, and many rulers had sought his counsel in order to better govern their own kingdoms. *Was this the intent of the Queen of Seven?* Each ruler had brought gifts of silver, gold, garments, armor, spices, horses, and mules. He wondered what this queen would bring.

The Queen and the wise King Solomon chatted amiably as they strolled the luxurious grounds of his palace. As they made their way to the Temple, she shared all that was in her heart as though she had taken Solomon by the hand and entered the oracle of *HaMelech*. Solomon understood that he was standing in the presence of Wisdom: the revealer of hidden things and the source of his wisdom. To confirm the depth of his understanding, the Queen proposed difficult riddles and entreated him to solve them. She told him she had been sent to see if he had indeed received the heavenly wisdom and understood its meaning. She would report her findings to the court of the heavenly host.

As they toured the Temple complex, she was pleased with the workmanship of the Temple. It was eerily similar to her heavenly home. She was amazed that a work of such beauty and grandeur was built by human hands. The Queen of Seven observed the magnificence of King Solomon's daily table and the preparation of all the offerings of food. She was impressed with the apparel worn by Solomon's servants and the skillful management of the entire house. She expressed great admiration for all that Solomon had accomplished on earth as it was in heaven. She noted, with joy in her heart, how happy (*ashrei*) the people would be and how they would benefit from his wisdom. "Blessed be *Adonai* your G-d who took pleasure in you to put you on HIS throne so that you could be king for *Adonai* your G-d. Because of your G-d's love for Israel to establish them forever he has made you king over them to administer law and judgment."

Completely satisfied with what she had seen, a massive whirlwind now appeared, surrounded by radiant clouds of glory, to carry the Queen's chariot home. There would pass many more appointed times before she returned to her husband's earthly abode. On a day known only to *HaMelech*, she would return on the wings of the eastern wind to visit the one born King of the Jews — carrying with her frankincense, gold, and myrrh. This king, however, would be the one to rebuild and restore the Temple of G-d, his father, and Wisdom, his mother, for all eternity.

Wisdom Builds the House

> Wisdom has built herself a house; she has carved her seven pillars. She has prepared her food, spiced her wine, and she has set her table.
>
> (PROV. 9.1,2)

Who is Wisdom? For nearly six centuries, the ancient Hebrews saw her as a consort to G-d, the Queen of Heaven, and the Tree of Life. The Deuteronomists saw her as the noble wife who personified the Torah. The early Christians linked Wisdom to the Holy Spirit through *Yeshua's* immersion. The Jewish literature from the Second Temple Period alluded to Wisdom as the *Ruach Elohim*: the Spirit of G-d hovering over the waters "in the beginning" at creation. Wisdom was also an idiom for the bride who was the Holy Temple.

The *Zohar* (a mystical commentary on the Torah) asks, "What is the meaning of *beresheet*? It means 'with Wisdom,' the Wisdom on which the world is based!" A Targum states, "In the beginning Wisdom the Lord created..."(Targum *Neofitit*). King David asked, "How many are the things you [wisdom] have made. You made them all with wisdom" (Ps. 104.24). Early Jewish writings, in referring to Wisdom, declare, "He created me from the beginning before the world; the memorial of me shall never cease. In the Holy Tabernacle, I ministered before Him, moreover in Zion was I established" (Sirach 24.9,10).

Adonai made me [Wisdom] as the beginning of his way, the firſt of his ancient works. I was appointed before the world, before the ſtart, before the earth's beginnings. When I was brought forth, there were no ocean depths, no ſprings brimming with water. I was brought forth before the hills, before the mountains had settled in place. For me, every day was pure delight, as I played in his presence all the time, playing everywhere on his earth, my delights are with the sons of man.

(PROV. 8.22-25,30B-31)

Philo referred to the pillar of cloud, descending and resting at the entrance of the Tabernacle, as Wisdom. In time, the pillar of cloud became known as the *Shekinah* (indwelling presence). "I [Wisdom] came forth from the mouth of the Most High and as a mist I covered the earth" (Sirach 24.3). "A mist would ascend from the earth and it watered the whole surface of the ground" (Gen. 2.6). Mist, in Hebrew, can also mean a cloud of dust rising when ash is raked in the fire. "She [Wisdom] was the smoke of incense in the Tabernacle" (Sirach 24.15b). She is a queen seated on her own throne "in a pillar of clouds" next to the throne of Yahweh, the male biblical G-d (Deconick 2011: 6).

In the ANE, *Wisdom* was an architectural expression for building a house. ANE kings showed their wisdom by building temples and filling them with the necessities to provide for the kingdom. The wisdom of G-d in creation was regularly portrayed in architectural terms and in relationship to the number seven. "The Akitu sanctuary in Assyria had two sets of seven pillars and the pillars of Solomon's Temple (1 Kings 7.17) had seven meshwork decorations" (Fox 2000: 297). In ancient Mesopotamia, "building was a matter of divine command and

agency and of human imitation of the divine wisdom in building"
(Ed. Clifford 2007: 404).

> By employing building terminology in the Creation story,
> the priestly author has done nothing new, but has joined
> other biblical writers who describe the world as a building,
> the Creation as an act of building, and the Creator as a
> wise, knowledgeable and discerning architect.
>
> (HUROWITZ 1992: 242)

> By Wisdom a house is built, by understanding it is made
> secure and by knowledge its rooms are filled with all kinds
> of costly and precious pleasant possessions.
>
> (PROV. 24.3-4)

A house was built with wisdom that the deity or king passed
on to the builder. G-d gave Moses the design for the Tabernacle
from the cosmic Temple. He equipped Bezalel, the master craftsman (Ex. 31.1-5), with wisdom, understanding, and knowledge
of every kind of artistry by "filling" him with the *Ruach Elohim*
(Spirit of G-d). G-d gave King David the designs and plans for
the First Temple (1 Chron. 28.19) which David communicated
to his son, Solomon. Hiram (1 Kings 7.14) was his master builder — filled with wisdom, understanding, and skill. According to
Van Leeuwen:

> Craftsmanship or skill *in any area of human endeavor* lies at
> the heart of biblical wisdom because wisdom is a concept
> as wide and all encompassing as creation, which in ancient
> thought included culture.
>
> (ED. CLIFFORD 2007: 419)

Those who heard *Yeshua* teaching in the synagogue
asked, "What is this wisdom he has been given...isn't he

the carpenter/the son of the carpenter" (Mark 6.2)? Geza Vermes noted that the metaphorical use of "carpenter" is based on a Talmudic proverb in which the Aramaic noun for "carpenter" or "craftsman" means "a scholar or learned man" (1981: 21). *Yeshua* grew strong in Spirit and was filled with wisdom (Luke 2.40); this is temple language for building a house. He "increased in wisdom and stature and in favor with G-d and men" (52). Paul explained, "It is in Messiah that all the treasures of wisdom and knowledge are hidden" (Col. 2.3).

When King Belshazzar drank from the silver and gold cups which had been removed from the First Temple after being ransacked and destroyed by his father, Nebuchadnezzar, a mysterious inscription appeared on the palace wall. When those present lacked the wisdom required to understand the inscription, it was the queen mother who reminded the King — in reference to Daniel the prophet, "There is a man in your kingdom in whom is the spirit of the holy gods. In the days of your father, he was found to have light, discernment and wisdom, like the wisdom of the gods...he was found to have extraordinary spirit, knowledge, discernment and the ability to interpret dreams, unlock mysteries and solve knotty problems" (Dan. 5.11,12).

Solomon demonstrated his wisdom to the Queen of Sheba after the Temple was completed (1 Kings 9.25,10.1). A Midrash states, "Solomon's wisdom was the Holy Spirit guiding him" (*Beresheet Rabbah* 85). The Queen posed riddles on all manner of topics that required *wisdom* to solve. The book of Proverbs likely represents the teachings of *Batsheva* (Bathsheba), the queen mother (Prov. 31.1), to her son Solomon. The first chapter describes how the proverbs are for learning about wisdom and discipline, for understanding, for doing what is right and fair, and for knowledge and discretion. Those who are wise will become wiser still and will understand the proverbs, parables, obscure expressions, sayings, and riddles which represent the language of the kingdom and the world behind the veil. The riddles are wisdom that emanated from the throne of the King.

> Yet there is a wisdom that we are speaking to those who are mature enough for it. But it is not the wisdom of this world or of this world's leaders, who are in the process of passing away. On the contrary we are communicating a secret wisdom from G-d that has been hidden until now but which, before history began, G-d had decreed would bring us glory.
>
> (1 CO. 2.6,7)

The book of Proverbs is filled with the biblical principles necessary to build a successful and prosperous home. Van Leeuwen also suggested that building a house/temple was a way to understand wisdom, creation, and divine activity (Ed. Clifford 2007: 404).

> For she [Wisdom] teaches self-control and understanding, righteousness and courage...she knows the things of old and divines the things to come: She understands subtleties of speeches and interpretations of dark saying: She foresees signs and wonders and the issues of seasons and times.
>
> (WISDOM OF SOLOMON 8.7B-8)

To listen to Wisdom, to live within her house, to partake of her food and wine, are different ways of envisioning a lifetime of learning.

> (FOX 2000: 297)

Will the Real Holy Spirit Please Stand Up!

Wisdom found no place where she might dwell; then a dwelling place was assigned her in the heavens. Wisdom went forth to make her dwelling among the children of men, and found no dwelling place: Wisdom returned to her place and took her seat among the angels.

(1 ENOCH 42.1,2)

The Holy Spirit is the Wisdom among women who builds her house (Prov. 14.1). To the ancients she was the mother goddess, Wisdom, and co-creator of the cosmic Temple. To the Deuteronomists she was the personification of the Torah (feminine noun). The Bible speaks of her in glowing terms: she delivered from transgression. She gave strength and dominion to Israel — delivering them from their oppressors. She saved the earth from the flood. She guided Israel in the wilderness and became their covering by day and their light by night. So, what does the Holy Spirit mean for us today?

Our culture was once positively influenced by a Judeo-Christian tradition in which biblical values were the guiding principles for living. Today the "world" is void of any common sense, and politically correct speech has evolved from the absurd to the outright dangerous. It is as though our world is suffering from extreme psychosis. The driving force behind decision making is based on irrational emotion instead of strong mental acumen. Wrong thinking leads to wrong actions which leads to devastating consequences. Political leaders have abandoned all vestiges of wisdom and have become Proverb's infamous foolish harlot — hating biblical wisdom and knowledge. We see the clash of two competing belief systems: wisdom versus worldly foolishness. Those who reject wisdom have lost their ability to discern between good and evil and have replaced one with the other. They have become blind, deaf, and unable to understand. They are fools who despise wisdom.

US Supreme Court Justice Antonin Scalia said it best

in a speech to the Knights of Columbus Council in Baton Rouge: "G-d assumed from the beginning that the wise of the world would view Christians as fools...and He has not been disappointed. If I have brought any message today, it is this: Have the courage to have your wisdom regarded as stupidity. Be fools for Christ. And have the courage to suffer the contempt of the sophisticated world."

It is the fear of the Lord that is the beginning of Wisdom (Prov. 1.7).

> For *Adonai* gives wisdom; from his mouth comes knowledge and understanding. He stores up common sense for the upright, is a shield to those whose conduct is blameless; in order to guard the courses of justice and preserve the way of those faithful to him. Then you will understand righteousness, justice, fairness and every good path. For wisdom will enter your heart, knowledge will be enjoyable for you, discretion will watch over you, and discernment will guard you. They will save you from the way of evil...
>
> (PROV. 2.6-12A)

The ministry of the Holy Spirit is manifested through the exercise of biblical wisdom. The Spirit moves in response to our obedience to the Word of G-d. The Spirit is not a feeling or an emotional high. The Spirit cannot be manipulated by wishful thinking, hoping, and dreaming. The Spirit is not some ethereal force leading us aimlessly without our permission. A "move" of the Spirit is not represented by excessive babbling, laughing hysterically, falling down on the floor, or advancing "revelations" that violate G-d's natural laws. What does it really mean to be led by the Spirit, to listen to the Spirit, to be filled with the Spirit, and to walk in the Spirit?

Often we act as though the Spirit was made in *our* image and likeness, but the Spirit was involved in the Creation. She brought forth new life in the same way a mother brings forth a child. The Spirit is often compared to a mother bird who builds her house/temple. A mother teaches, trains, instructs, guides, nurtures, comforts, and protects her children. She passes customs and family traditions to succeeding generations. She molds and shapes character so her children will produce good fruit. She equips her children with knowledge and wisdom so they are filled with every good thing. She discerns and judges fairly; she preserves the integrity of her house. This is the ministry of the Holy Spirit. To be filled with the Holy Spirit is to be filled with wisdom; this is temple dedication language. To blaspheme the Spirit is to reject Wisdom, the mother. To be immersed in the Spirit is to be filled with wisdom, knowledge, and understanding — like the master craftsmen who built the Tabernacle and the Temple — so we can build our homes, our communities, and our nation. A house is built when its members follow the commandments and principles that are laid out in the Bible. The same holds true for the Body of Messiah which Paul described as a temple. When obeyed, Wisdom is the instruction manual allowing for the smooth operation of the house. Rebellion against these principles will build a different kind of house — and ultimately a different kind of nation.

This life is about making choices that bring either life or death. There is no middle ground. We either build up the house or we tear it down. To be filled with the Spirit is to be filled with the wisdom to make good choices. Being filled with wisdom produces good fruit (love, joy, peace, patience, kindness, goodness, faithfulness, gentleness, and self-control). "But the wisdom from above is, first of all, pure then peaceful, kind, open to reason, full of mercy and good fruits, without partiality and without hypocrisy" (James 3.17). Walking in the Spirit necessitates discipline and obedience. Adam and Eve were given freewill to choose which fruit they would eat. Eating from the Tree of Life *would have* brought them godly wisdom for all eternity; eating from the Tree of Knowledge brought about the destruction of their house. Foolishness, which is a lack of wisdom, always leads to death. Obedience bears fruit and births abundant life.

The Body of Messiah is a temple that is patterned after the creation. Creation is built upon the union of male and female elements. The key to building a healthy, functioning house is to strike the right balance between the two. Unfortunately, that balance remains elusive. Many "religious communities" have marginalized women. They have shut off their primary role in the body of Messiah, which is to teach, and have instead given it solely to men. The societal culture, on the other hand, has marginalized men — relinquishing their role, in both the home and the culture, to women. This has led to a completely dysfunctional society. This imbalance will produce very little in the way of good fruit. Rebuilding a house means restoring the proper balance between men and women. The arrival of Messiah and the final redemption will permanently correct the imbalance between masculine and feminine that has existed since Adam and Eve first sinned. This is the "good news"; *Yeshua* the Messiah came to restore creation to its original state.

Wisdom will not enter a heart that is bent on evil or dwell in a body that is pledged to sin. And so G-d declared, "Repent when I reprove — I will pour out my Spirit to you" (Prov. 1.23). He declared, "I will give you a new heart and put a new spirit inside you. "I will put my Spirit inside you and cause you to live by my laws" (Ezek. 36.27). A regenerated heart is all that is needed for wisdom to rebuild the house and produce new life. Has your heart been regenerated?

It is to us, however, that G-d has revealed these things. How? Through the Spirit! For the Spirit probes all things, even the profoundest depths of G-d. For who knows the inner workings of a person except the person's own spirit inside him? So too no one knows the inner workings of G-d except G-d's Spirit. Now we have not received the spirit of the world but the Spirit of G-d, so that we might understand the things G-d has so freely given us.

(1 CO. 2.10-12)

CHAPTER SIX

SEVEN AND THE TEMPLE

*At the end of every seven years, during the festival
of Sukkot in the year of sh'mittah, when all Israel
have come to appear in the presence of Adonai at the
place he will choose, you are to read this Torah before
all Israel, so that they can hear it. Assemble (hakhel)
the people — the men, the women, the little ones and
the foreigners you have in your towns — so that they
can hear, learn, fear Adonai your G-d and take care
to obey all the words of this Torah: and so that their
children, who have not known, can hear and learn to
fear Adonai your G-d, for as long as you live in the
land you are crossing the Yarden to possess.*

(Deut. 31.10-13)

The septennial *Hakhel* (from the root *kahal* meaning a gathering) was likely the backdrop for Nehemiah chapter eight. This event found *all* the people gathered, once every seven years, to hear the words of the scroll of Moses. The following vignette describes how the *Hakhel* may have been celebrated:

Jews from around the empire steadily streamed into the city of Jerusalem for the seven day festival of *Sukkot*. As the day dawned with brilliant blue skies, the pilgrims made their way up the steep ascent to the city singing the ancient songs: "For the Lord has chosen Zion; He has desired it for His dwelling place: This is My resting place forever; Here I will dwell, for I have desired it" (Ps. 132 NKJV). Voices reverberated loudly throughout the narrow canyon where the steadily approaching caravans overflowed with joy and freshly harvested foodstuffs: grapes, figs, dates, olives, and pomegranates. When they reached the city's edge, the sight of the Holy Temple in the distance — a towering white crystal palace glittering in the morning sun — further electrified the already jubilant crowd.

This *Sukkot* was special for it included the *Hakhel*: the ceremony where every man, woman, and child of Israel, along with "the stranger within their gates," assembled in the Courtyard of the Women to hear the King read from the Torah of Moses. The *Hakhel* was celebrated once every seven years, at *Sukkot*, in the year following the *sh'mittah* or sabbatical year.

With the ashes from the morning's offering still smoldering, a group of young priests entered the Temple courtyard — walking in lockstep towards the great altar. They carried giant willow branches that made a swishing sound as they were rustled by the morning breeze. Earlier that day, the same priests had hiked down to Motza, a town at the foot of the city of Jerusalem, to cut the branches which they now placed around the base of the altar. The willow heads formed a miniature *sukkah* — tenting the altar in celebration of the Feast. The priests paraded around the altar shouting, "We beseech you, O Lord, please save us!" On the last day of *Sukkot, Hoshannah Rabbah* (the day of the great salvation), they would circle the altar seven times to memorialize Israel's conquest of Jericho.

A number of priests who had dispersed throughout the streets of Jerusalem began blowing silver trumpets to call the nation to assemble. Other priests were putting the finishing touches on the four lampstands that had been erected in the Court of the Women in preparation for the evening's lighting. A cedar wood platform, specially constructed for the *Hakhel* ceremony, was placed in the center of the courtyard between the lampstands. As the shofar blasts pierced the quiet of the Temple precincts, worshippers politely pushed through the throng in order to gain a better view. A final blast heralded the entrance of the king who made his way up the platform's makeshift steps to take his place in front of the temporary throne. The Temple administrator, tasked with carrying the Scroll of Moses, climbed the steps behind the king. Standing before the crowd, he passed the ornate scroll to the deputy high priest who in turn handed it to the high priest. Finally, with great fanfare accompanied by thunderous applause, the high priest formally presented the scroll to the king who carefully unrolled the calfskin parchment from its housing called the *Etz Chaim* (Tree of Life).

The king sat, cleared his throat, took a deep breath, and began to speak to the nation. (Some in the crowd remembered that King Agrippa had stood while reading from the Torah. The sages at that time saw standing as a sign of respect for G-d and for the nation.) In a loud, booming voice, the King recited the special benedictions. Then, after reading from various portions of the book of Deuteronomy, he spoke the eight final blessings — seven of which were recited by the high priest on the Day of Atonement, "...I beseech you, O Lord, that the Holy Temple should remain standing...blessed are you who sanctifies the *kohanim*...Help, O G-d, your nation Israel for your nation needs salvation."

The king's words hung in the air long after he had finished reading — stirring the hearts of his people. They thought back to the time when their forefathers had gathered at the Tabernacle in Shiloh upon entering the land of Israel — when Joshua son of Nun had spoken to the people.

Later that evening, as the king reflected back over the day's events, he was reminded that he was not just the political and military leader of the nation. He was G-d's "anointed one." As such, he was responsible for the spiritual well- being of his people.

In 1945, the first *Hakhel* ceremony since the destruction of the Second Temple was held at the *Yeshurun* synagogue in Jerusalem. Over the next sixty years, a number of smaller ceremonies would be held in the city. It was the *Hakhel* ceremony held sixty-three years later, however, that some recognized as the first sign of the redemption. On the second day of *Sukkot*, in the year 2008/5769, a *Hakhel* was held on the Temple Mount for the first time in nearly 2000 years. Preparations had been made in secret over many months. Though six hundred or so were prevented from entering due to intentionally slow security checks, four hundred worshippers stood on the Temple Mount and read passages from Deuteronomy. Later that day, in another location in Jerusalem, the Temple Institute proudly displayed some of their accomplishments from the previous year: newly fashioned silver trumpets, the golden crown of the high priest, and garments for lay priests. The day concluded with the unveiling of the brass laver — used for the sanctification of the priests in the Temple. Silver trumpets were blown as five prominent *kohanim* (priests) prepared to read from the Torah scroll. The newly made golden crown was placed on the head of one priest. The *Hakhel* ceremony that year was seen as a date with destiny; it signified to those present that the Messiah would soon appear.

Seven in the Bible

And the seventh — you found favor in it and sanctified it! Most coveted of days, You called it, a remembrance of the Act of Creation.

(*Holiness of the Day* PRAYER FROM THE *Amidah* FOR THE SABBATH)

Like the *Hakhel*, many ceremonies in the Temple were structured around the number seven: a number traditionally associated with enthronement and temple dedication rituals celebrated at ANE New Year's festivals. Students of the Bible generally identify seven with perfection or completion. More significantly to the ANE mind, however, the number seven represented the building and dedication of a temple and the crowning of a king. "One must speak of ordering the cosmos in terms of seven even as the construction of the microcosm must be according to the sacred number" (L. Fisher 1963: 40-41). "Creation in Genesis…is described as a temple; it is constructed as an ancient Near Eastern temple would be constructed" (Kline, 1999).

To understand the significance of the number seven, it is helpful to examine temple building in the context of ANE creation myths — which reveal many similarities with the creation account in Genesis.

Enuma Elish, the Babylonian creation myth (a version from Ashurbanipal's library dates back to the seventh century BCE), was recorded on clay tablets called the Seven Tablets of Creation. *Enuma Elish* tells of the creation of the world, Marduk's victory over Tiamat, and how Marduk ultimately became king of the gods. This account was recited annually at the Akitu: the Babylonian New Year which was celebrated in the spring month of Nissanu. (Note: the dedication of the Tabernacle of Moses took place in the spring on the first day of the Hebrew month, Nisan.)

Enuma Elish begins with creation in a formless state — similar to the Genesis account — out of which emerged two primary gods: the male Apsu (the sweet waters) and the female Tiamat (the bitter waters). At the mouth of the Tigris and Euphrates, the original site of Mesopotamian civilization, sweet and salt waters mingled to create life. The union of these two entities gave birth to the younger gods. During the New Year's festival, the statue of Marduk was removed from his temple and paraded through the streets of the city as the *Enuma Elish* was chanted.

ANE cultures tied their New Year's rituals to a completed temple. The annual celebration featured enthronement ceremonies for the newly "anointed king." New Year's festivals also celebrated the revivification or resurrection of the king and the marriage of the god to his consort. "The rededication of the Temple would signal the resumption of cosmic union and harmony" (Lundquist 2008: xiv). There are a number of similarities between these ANE New Year's rituals and *Rosh Hashanah* (head of the year) or the Jewish New Year. Celebrated on the first day of the seventh month, this feast is commonly known in Christian circles as the Feast of Trumpets. Themes surrounding the ancient Jewish New Year included the wedding ceremony, the king's enthronement, the meting out of judgment, and the resurrection of the king.

ANE Scholar Victor Hurowitz discovered more than forty instances where the number seven was connected to ANE temple building, dedication and enthronement rituals. He noted examples from the Gudea Cylinders (1992: 38-59) which depict temple building in ancient Sumer. Dated at around 2125 BCE, these cylinders were written in cuneiform and describe the temple of the Babylonian/Sumerian rain and fertility god, Ningirsu, who was the patron deity over Girsu (Lagesh). The cylinders, made by King Gudea of Lagesh, were found in 1877 during excavations at Tell Telloh, Iraq (ancient Girsu). They contain the historical record of the construction of Ningirsu's temple: Eninnu (House of the Fifty). Additionally, they describe the annual New Year's enthronement ceremony of the divine king and queen of Lagash.

Cylinder A describes the plan for the temple's design — given to King Gudea by his god, Ningirsu, who appeared to him in a dream. The inscriptions show how the human king and the divine god interacted in the construction of the sacred temple. Like King Solomon, Gudea imported the temple's materials — wood, metal, bitumen, blocks of stone, etc. — from faraway places.

Cylinder B recounts the dedication of the temple in the spring — describing the enthronement of the divine couple as well as their sacred marriage. Fertility rites accompanied the ceremony and guaranteed the renewal of life from inside the inner sanctum. The wedding signified new life for the parched land, and the enthronement of the king symbolized the resurrection of the deceased god. In the ancient world, building, re-building and/or restoring a temple was *the* most notable accomplishment of a ruler.

We are introduced to a similar seven-day temple building pattern in the first verse of Genesis. Seven Hebrew words are translated: "In the beginning G-d made the heavens and the earth." Seven, or *sheva*, also means an oath. Rabbi Hirsch said, "An oath obligates a person through everything that was made in the seven days of creation." Traditionally, an oath imposed a special obligation on the person who made the verbal pledge. When spoken out loud, the promise became binding, and so failing to keep an oath brought a curse on the one who broke the promise. An oath was sacred, and over time specific penalties were imposed upon those who swore falsely. Oaths were an important part of Israel's national life in terms of lawsuits, affairs of state, and everyday life. It became common practice to confirm an oath between parties with seven verbal declarations. (Solomon spoke seven petitions at the dedication of the First Temple). It has been suggested that "In the beginning" G-d was making a binding oath with His creation in the presence of two witnesses: heaven and earth.

> They are strong through His *oath*: and the heaven was suspended before the world was created, and forever. And through it the earth was founded upon the water, and from the secret recesses of the mountains come beautiful waters, from the creation of the world unto eternity. And through that *oath* the sea was created and as its foundation he set for it the sand against the time of anger, and it dare not pass beyond it from the creation of the world unto eternity. And through the *oath* are the depths made fast...and through the *oath* the sun and moon complete their course...and through the *oath* the stars complete their course and He calls them by their names and they answer Him from eternity to eternity.
>
> (1 ENOCH 69.16-21)

The seventh day, *Shabbat* (sabbath), was the apex of Creation. When G-d "rested" on the seventh it meant His cosmic Temple was finished. It was filled with "furniture" (sun, moon, stars, fish, birds, animals etc.) and fully operational. Philo said the seventh day meant that unity was restored. In Leviticus *Rabbah*, the number seven was precious to the world above (29.10).

> And I know not if any one would be able to celebrate the nature of the number seven in adequate terms, since it is superior to every form of expression.
>
> (PHILO *On the Creation* 90)

On the seventh day, the type of work necessary to *build*

the creation Temple was replaced with work called *avodah* (service): the liturgical services of the Temple performed by the priests. Adam was assigned to "work" and "guard" the garden sanctuary. Work referred to the ritual services and ceremonies he performed as high priest. "Genesis depicts the world as a macro-temple and humanity as created for liturgical worship as cosmic priests on earth" (Morrow 2009).

Many sevens are found throughout the Bible. A good example is the festival cycle outlined in Leviticus (23) which begins with the Sabbath: the seventh day. This is followed by the season of Passover in the spring with its seven-day celebration. *Shavuot* (meaning sevens), or the Feast of Weeks, is the actual conclusion to Passover and is celebrated seven weeks later. *Sukkot*, observed in the fall, is another seven-day festival.

Solomon's Temple was completed in seven years and dedicated at *Sukkot* (in the seventh month) over two periods of seven days. Solomon's dedication speech included seven declarations (1 Kings 8.31-53). The manufacture of the priestly garments (Ex. 39) and the construction of the Tabernacle (Ex. 40) were described in patterns of seven. Wedding and marriage rituals were connected to the number seven. Jacob worked for two periods of seven years in order to marry Leah and Rachel.

The Spirit, described as "sevenfold" (Rev. 1.4), would rest on the tender shoot that came forth from the stump of Jesse (Is. 11.1,2): the root and offspring of King David (Rev. 22.16). G-d promised to equip this shoot with the seven spirits: The Spirit of the Lord, Wisdom, Understanding, Counsel, Might, Knowledge, and Fear. "In these seven forms the Holy Spirit descended upon the second David" (Keil & Delitzsch 2011: 182-183).

The number seven is also connected to ceremonies related to the laws of ritual purity, to the altar offerings, to birth and death cycles, and to periods of judgment. Seven is *the* framework for the entire agricultural, civilian, judicial, and religious life of Israel — all in the context of temple building, dedication and enthronement.

The Seventh Day

> *And completed (kallah) were the heavens and the earth and all their hosts. G-d completed (kallah) on the seventh day His work, which He had done and He ceased on the seventh day from all His work which He had done. G-d blessed the seventh day and He set apart it because on it He ceased from His work which G-d created to make.*
>
> (GEN. 2.1 SCHOTTENSTEIN ED.)

> *To the G-d who rested from all works and who on the seventh Day was elevated and sat on the Throne of His Glory. With splendor He enwrapped the Day of Contentment (He declared the Sabbath a day of delight).*
>
> (La'el PRAYER FOR THE SABBATH)

The seventh was a day of rest meaning it was a day related to temple dedication, enthronement, and marriage. Rest in the ANE meant the god was now enthroned in his temple as a victor over all his enemies. The "waters of chaos" represented G-d's enemies. (This is the framework for the story of Noah's ark.) In his article, "Sabbath, Temple and the Enthronement of the Lord" Moshe Weinfeld emphasizes this connection stating that victory by the god over his enemies resulted in a day dedicated to his enthronement. In the biblical creation account, G-d's rest signified that His throne was established on the seventh day. The Song of the Sea (Ex. 15) concludes with G-d's holy abode as "the place" and "the sanctuary" established in the mountain of G-d's heritage. This was sung after Pharaoh and his army drowned in the depths of the sea.

The Song is referenced again in Revelation (15) where those who have defeated the beast are standing by the sea of glass singing the Song of Moses before the throne. "Rest" from one's enemies denotes the establishment of a "throne of kingship."

In the Bible, G-d "rested" from His labor and "dwelled" in His Sanctuary on the seventh day. Many of the *Shabbat* (Sabbath) prayers affirm G-d as King seated on the "throne of His glory." Psalm 132 (8), an enthronement psalm and one of the fifteen Songs of Ascent, declares, "Arise *Adonai* to your resting place you and your ark of your glory...this is my rest forever." Sigmund Mowinckle, in his book, *The Psalms in Israel's Worship*, identified enthronement psalms for the Sabbath that were part of the liturgy of the Second Temple: Psalms 92-99, 29, 90, 19. Psalm 93 states, "*Adonai* is king, robed in majesty; *Adonai* is robed, girded with strength...Your throne was established long ago; you have existed forever." Psalm 29 says, "*Adonai* sits enthroned above the flood! *Adonai* sits enthroned as king forever!" In Psalm 95, "For *Adonai* is a great G-d, a great king greater than all gods." Psalm 97 notes, "*Adonai* is king, let the earth rejoice!" Psalm 99 declares, "*Adonai* is king; let the peoples tremble. He sits enthroned on the *K'ruvim* (cherubim)."

Rosh HaShanah (meaning Head of the Year) is a high Sabbath celebrated on the first day of the seventh month (Num. 29.1). The liturgy for this day is filled with enthronement language. Psalm 24 declares, "Lift up your heads, you gates! Lift them up, everlasting doors, so that the glorious king can enter. Who is He, this glorious king? *Adonai* strong and mighty; *Adonai* mighty in battle." Psalm 47 states, "*Adonai Elyon* is awesome, a great king over all the earth. G-d goes up to shouts of acclaim, *Adonai* to a blast on the shofar... sing praises to our king, sing praises! For G-d is king of all the earth...G-d sits on his holy throne."

"G-d sanctified the seventh day because on it he rested from all his work which G-d created and made" (Gen. 2.3). In the first chapter of Genesis, two types of work are implied: the work involved in building the Temple and the work required to perform the Temple services. Mankind was the bridge between the two. It was said that man's service on the Sabbath restored the universe to its original glory. The Sabbath was also declared *Kadosh*, holy, in that G-d blessed the seventh day and set it apart for a particular function. With this function came certain restrictions: the prohibition against regular work and the lighting of fire.

Setting apart the Sabbath from the other six working days brought supernatural blessing to the community. It was as though the "veil" that hung between the six days and the seventh was removed every *Shabbat*. This signified a leaving of "this world" in order to enter the "world outside of time": the Holy of Holies and the throne room of the King. In the Ugaritic Ba'al myth, a fire burned for six days and then stopped on the seventh as Ba'al rejoiced and took up residence in his temple. The throne of Ba'al was called the "throne of rest." In the sanctuary of the god El was the "seat of rest." When El placed his feet on his footstool, he declared, "Now I will sit and rest" (Weinfeld 1981: 504).

> But after the whole world had been completed according to the perfect nature of the number six, the Father hallowed the day following, the seventh, praising it, and calling it holy. For that day is the festival, not of one city or one country, but of all the earth; a day which alone it is right to call the day of festival for all people, and the birthday of the world.
>
> (PHILO *On the Creation* 89,90)

Each Sabbath, the words, "and thus were completed the heaven and earth and all their hosts" are recited (Gen. 2.1-3). The seventh day was the completion (*kallah*) of the heavens and earth, and the number seven is related to the Tabernacle (Ex. 40.2) and Solomon's Temple (1 Kings 7.40).

Only when Solomon came and built the Temple would the Holy One, blessed be He, say: 'Now the work of creation, heaven and earth is completed: Now all the work...is completed.' This was why he was called Solomon (whose name means he who is destined to finish) because it was through the work of his hands that the Holy One, blessed be He, completed the work of the six days of creation.

(WEINFELD 1981: 504N)

The Hebrew word for bride, *kallah*, is closely associated with the idea of completion. This may be why the wedding became an integral part of the Sabbath's rituals. The sages say that on the night of the Sabbath the king is joined to the bride and from this union the souls of the righteous are produced. "The heavens declare the glory of G-d...in them he places a tent for the sun which comes out like a bridegroom from the bridal chamber" (Ps. 19.2,5b). The Zohar asks why the Sabbath is called *kallah* or a bride. The answer is this: the Sabbath is G-d's spouse (II, 63b). "The community of Israel is called a Sabbath queen for she is G-d's spouse" (Patterson 2005: 150).

The custom of receiving the queen takes place on the eve of *Shabbat*. "Rabbi *Yannai* donned his robes on Sabbath eve and exclaimed, 'Come, O bride, Come, O bride'" (BT *Shabbat* 119a)! During the Sabbath, the Divine Presence — the *Shekinah* of G-d — is welcomed into every home. The *Shekinah* is a symbol of G-d's bride. The eternal hope of the Jewish people is the return of the Divine Presence to the Temple after their long and often bitter exile. Perhaps this is linked to the Spirit and the Bride in Revelation (22.17).

Due in large part to their celebration of the *Shabbat*, the Jewish people have remained a distinct nation — separated from the cultures around them. In times of persecution, this has made them an easy and an identifiable target. In spite of this, they have maintained their identity over many millennia.

The *Shabbat* reminds us that G-d is faithful, that He is enthroned in His Holy Temple, and that He dwells among all His people. It is a day when the entire community steps into the "world outside of time" and worships at His throne. It is a day when relationships are nurtured and families are rejuvenated. At home we eat, pray, share, sing, and study together. In doing so, we become part of His Holy House. One purpose for the Sabbath, the seventh day, is to protect and preserve the family. This is especially true as we see the days grow more evil and the world continue its downward slide into chaos and tribulation.

The Bride or the Harlot

> Six things preceded the creation of the world. Some were created, some arose in thought to be created: The Torah and the Throne of Glory were created...The patriarchs, Israel, the Temple, and the name of the Messiah arose in thought to be created...The Temple, from where? As it is stated: "A glorious throne exalted from the beginning is the place of our sanctuary.
>
> (GEN. *Rabbah* 1.4; JER. 17.12)

The book of Revelation is an ANE temple text filled with colorful, imaginative language and built around the number seven: seven spirits, seven congregations, seven stars, seven years, seven trumpets, seven bowls, seven seals, seven eyes, seven horns, seven heads, seven plagues, seven angels, seven thunders, etc. These symbols were likely understood by those of the first century; however, much of that understanding has been lost. Proper context is key. Our lack of knowledge regarding the Temple often leads to wild assumptions.

To ancient minds, the number seven signified not only a time of rest but also a period of judgment. In the story of Noah, the waters of the flood came on the earth "after seven days." Pharaoh's dream of sickly cows and scorched grain prophesied a seven-year period of judgment. G-d struck the Nile River as a judgment on Egypt after seven days. Judah was taken captive by the Babylonian empire for a period of seventy years because they neglected the Sabbatical year (for a period of seventy years).

The seven years in the book of Revelation, often referred to as "the great tribulation," represent both a time of rest in the heavenly realms (the world outside of time) and a time of judgment on the earth below. Two key players emerge: the "bride" and the "harlot" (as in Proverbs). Both represent the spiritual nature of the Temple leadership — in particular the high priest. The bride was originally Wisdom and the Tree of Life who symbolized the purity of G-d's House. The Tree of Knowledge, on the other hand, was Folly (or the harlot) who prostituted herself with G-d's enemies and corrupted the sanctity of the Temple environment. The bride was *kadosh*: holy, dedicated, and set apart. The harlot was *kedushah* (from the same root): one who dedicated herself to many "lovers" instead of remaining faithful to one. The city of Jerusalem, together with the Temple and its leadership, were at different times described by the prophets as being either a pure bride or a polluted harlot.

"The book of Revelation, like the Temple Scroll, implies that the Temple and the city [Jerusalem] coincide. The heavenly city is both city and Temple" (Barker 2000: 323). Rashi said the tent of meeting had "the appearance of a modest bride who has her face covered by a veil" (commentary on Ex. 26.9).

And it came to pass while I was talking with her, behold, her face upon a sudden shined exceedingly, and her countenance glistered, so that I was afraid of her, and mused what it might be. And, behold, suddenly she made a great cry very fearful: so that the earth shook at the noise of the woman. And I looked, and, behold, the woman appeared unto me no more, but there was a city built, and a large place showed itself from the foundations.

(2 ESDRAS 10.25-27)

And the city which G-d desired, this he made more brilliant than stars and sun and moon, and he provided ornament and made a Holy Temple, exceedingly beautiful in its fair shrine...

(SIBYLLINE ORACLES 5.420)

The First Temple had been a harlot because of the worship of foreign gods; the second had been a harlot because foreign money was accepted for rebuilding and yet many who worshipped the Lord were excluded; and Herod's rebuilt temple city was a harlot who had grown rich with the wealth of her wantonness.

(BARKER 2000: 279)

Barker suggested that the destruction of the great city, Jerusalem, and the Temple, had more to do with their wealth and the economic situation in Judea during the first century than anything else. The Second Temple was rife with corruption mainly because of the actions of a few high priests who exerted immense economic control over the Temple institution through usury, extortion, bribery, and graft. Their actions corrupted the house: a pattern that was repeated throughout Israel's history.

The Qumran scrolls mention a "wicked high priest" who had aligned himself with the foreign power of the day: Rome. He was the "great dragon" (Rev. 12.15) who pursued the fleeing woman (the Qumran community) to the wilderness while spewing water from his mouth in order to sweep her away in the flood. The "land" (temple building language) came to her rescue, and the male child she birthed was the Messiah: the rightful high priest of the heavenly Tabernacle. He would restore G-d's

House: the pure bride without spot or wrinkle.

Isaiah the prophet understood the corrupt nature of the city/Temple when he said, "How the faithful city has become a whore! Once she that was filled with justice, righteousness lodged in her" (Is. 1.21). She was the harlot who became corrupt through her commerce (Rev. 18) and engaged in unholy alliances with foreign empires. Eventually the city/Temple was identified with the empire of Babylon—not so much for her worship of pagan gods but rather because the Temple was built using foreign (Persian) money by those who returned from Babylon (Barker 2000: 282).

The book of Lamentations describes the judgment, and the subsequent destruction, that fell upon the city and Temple as a consequence for playing the harlot: "How lonely lies the city that once thronged with people! Once great among the nations, now she is like a widow" (1.1)! "Not one of her lovers is there to comfort her" (1.2b). "All splendor has departed from the Daughter of Zion" (1.6). "Jerusalem sinned grievously; therefore she has become unclean" (1.8). "I called out to my lovers, but they let me down. My *kohanim* (priests) and leaders perished in the city" (1.19). The harlot joined herself to foreigners and committed adultery with the kings of the earth. The great harlot was impure and her impurity polluted the whole earth (Rev. 18.1-4). It is likely the Essenes, and many of the early Christians, desired a "new Jerusalem" which meant a return to the original garden sanctuary.

> For, look! I create new heavens and a new earth; past things will not be remembered…so be glad and rejoice forever in what I am creating; for look! I am making *Yerushalayim* (Jerusalem) a joy, and her people a delight. I will rejoice in *Yerushalayim* and take joy in my people. The sound of weeping will no longer be heard in it…
>
> (IS. 65.17-19)

The harlot in Revelation was seated on many waters, on seven mountains, and on a scarlet beast which are all examples of temple imagery. In the ANE world, a temple was built on dry ground over the waters of chaos. In this case, the temple on the "hill" became the harlot's bed (Is. 57.7). The raging waters signified G-d's enemies. Jeremiah described the invading Philistine armies in this way: "Water is rising out of the north, it will become a flooding stream, flooding the land and all that is in it the city and its inhabitants" (Jer. 47.1,2). He also prophesied that Babylon would ultimately be destroyed: "The sea has flooded *Bavel*, overwhelmed her with its raging waves" (51.42).

The prophet Ezekiel (chapters 16 and 23) also painted a graphic picture of unfaithful Jerusalem as she pursued "other lovers" and indulged in adulterous behavior. She committed "fornication" with foreigners — Egyptians, Assyrians, and Babylonians — like the harlot of Revelation. The beast was likely the ruler (at the time of Revelation) of the foreign empire with which she committed adultery. Barker commented that it was "Rome's throne" that had been set up inside the Temple. Symbols like the "image of the beast" and "the harlot" would, over time, take on different interpretations based on evolving political realities and players.

You do all these things behaving like a shameless whore… here is a wife who commits adultery who goes to bed with strangers instead of her husband…you give gifts to all your lovers, you bribe them to come to you from all over the place and have sex with you.

(EZEK. 16.30,32)

Like mother, like daughter. Yes, you are your mother's daughter, who despises her husband and children; you are the sister of your sisters, who despises her husband

and children; your mother was a *Hitti* and your father an *Emori*. Moreover your older sister *Shomron* (Samaria), who lives at your left, she and her daughters; and your younger sister, living at your right, is Sodom with her daughters.

(EZEK. 16.44)

For here is what *Adonai Elohim* says: I will do to you as you have done — you treated the oath with contempt by breaking the covenant. Nevertheless, I will remember the covenant I made with you when you were a girl and will establish an everlasting covenant with you.

(EZEK.16.59)

The harlot was dressed in the manner of the Temple. She was clothed in purple and scarlet and adorned with gold, jewels, and pearls (Rev. 17.4) — like the robes of the high priest and the curtain. Josephus described the outer veil in front of the Great Gate of the Second Temple as a "Babylonian curtain, embroidered with blue, and fine linen and scarlet and purple and of a contexture that was truly wonderful" (*Wars of the Jews* 5.212). The breastplate of the high priest was made of pure gold and precious stones (Barker 2000: 284). A Targum from Isaiah said of the high priest, "He has covered me with the upper garment of righteousness, like a bridegroom who is happy in his bride-chamber, and like the high priest who decks himself with his robes, and like a bride who is adorned with her jewels" (61.10b). The Roman Empire housed the high priest's garments and released them only at festivals (Josephus *Antiquities of the Jews* 15.403; 18.93,94). The harlot had become the consort of the beast.

But you put your trust in your own beauty and began prostituting yourself because of your fame, soliciting everyone passing by and accepting all comers. You took your clothes and used them to decorate with bright colors the high places you made for yourself, and there you continue prostituting yourself.

(EZEK. 16.15,16)

Then I bathed you in water, washed the blood off you, and anointed you with oil. I also clothed you with an embroidered gown, gave you fine leather sandals to wear, put a fine linen headband on your head and covered you with silk. I gave you jewelry to wear: bracelets for your hands, a necklace for your neck, a ring for your nose, earrings for your ears and a beautiful crown for your head. Thus you were decked out in gold and silver; your clothing was of fine linen, silk and richly embroidered cloth...you grew increasingly beautiful — you were fit to be queen.

(EZEK. 16.9-14)

The harlot on earth is contrasted with the pure, undefiled bride dressed in fine white in heaven. Josephus described the Temple as built of white marble and cedar wood. She (city/Temple) was the beautiful bride prepared for her groom, the high priest. The "woman clothed with the sun" in Revelation (12) symbolizes the pure Temple, the heavenly Jerusalem, who brought forth a son from her union with the bridegroom. Temples in the ANE were built in an east/west orientation, based on the movement of the sun, and so with each sunrise the Temple looked as though it were being "dressed" in fine white garments.

The Song of Songs is likely an allegory describing the bride (Temple) with her lover (G-d/high priest) inside the wedding chamber called the "couch": the Holy of Holies. Rabbi *Akiva* declared, "The entire world is not worth as much as the day on which the Song of Songs was given to Israel; for all the Writings are holy, but the Song of Songs is the Holy of Holies." In the Songs, the "tents of Kedar" are dark and tanned (like the wilderness Tabernacle) and beautiful like the curtains of Solomon (1.5). The bride is a garden "locked up with a pool covered over" (4.12) and "an orchard with a garden fountain and spring of running water" (4.13,15). Eden, the garden sanctuary, was the original undefiled bride.

The Daughter of Zion was the city of Jerusalem that G-d promised to rebuild with precious stones (Is. 54.11-12). "Her maker is her husband, the Lord of hosts is his name" (Is 54.5). The woman, the bride, the daughter, and the mother, were all symbols for the restored city. Paul referred to the heavenly Temple as a mother: one who produces children. "The Jerusalem above is free and she is our mother" (Gal 4.26-27). The New Jerusalem was referred to as the heavenly city that brought forth sons. "Zion is the mother of us all. Jerusalem, the mother of us all, is overcome with grief and shame" (2 Esdras 10.7). "The Temple was her tent" (Lam. 2.4) but she has "become a widow. Once princess among provinces, she has become a vassal" (Lam. 1.1). "When a man has seen the death of his wife it is as though he had witnessed the destruction of the Temple" (BT *Sanhedrin* 22a).

> O Lord, my Lord, have I therefore come into the world to see the evil things of my mother? No my Lord. If I have found grace in your eyes, take away my spirit first that I may go to my fathers and I may not see the destruction of my mother. For from two sides I am hard pressed: I cannot resist you, but my soul also cannot behold the evil of my mother...For if you destroy your city and deliver up your country to those who hate us, how will the name of Israel be remembered again?
>
> (2 BARUCH 3.1-4)

The city/Temple bride was dressed in fine linen representative of wedding garments: white and pure like the high priest on the Day of Atonement. She wore a bridal veil that functioned like the curtain in front of the Holy of Holies. Jerusalem wearing beautiful garments signified that she was rebuilt of fine stone with foundations of sapphire, windows that shone with rubies, gates of garnet, and walls of gemstones (Is. 54.11-12). In Psalm 45, one of the royal wedding psalms according to Mowinckle, "The king's daughter looks splendid, attired in checker-work embroidered in gold. In brocade she will be led to the king." The psalm describes the high priest as a warrior — riding in the heavens with sword and fragrant robes to meet his bride (city/Temple) who is dressed as the queen.

> One of the seven angels having the seven bowls full of the seven plagues approached me and said, 'Come! I will show you the Bride, the Wife of the Lamb.' He carried me off in the Spirit to the top of a great, high mountain and showed me the holy city, *Yerushalayim*, coming down out of heaven from G-d. It had the *Shekinah* of G-d, so that its brilliance was like that of a priceless jewel, like a crystal-clear diamond.
>
> (REV. 21.9-11)

> Also I saw the holy city, New *Yerushalayim*, coming down out of heaven from G-d, prepared like a bride beautifully dressed for her husband.
>
> (REV. 21.2)

Temple language like this can be found throughout the Bible — especially in the prophets. There is such an overlay of imagery that oftentimes the symbols and language become confusing. It is difficult for our "modern" minds to accept that multiple things can be true at the same time. The Temple can represent the cosmos, the garden, the bride, Wisdom, a wife, Jerusalem, Israel, the community, and the family. Clearly the

Temple is much more than a physical building. And though there is no standing Temple, this does not mean the "church" has replaced it. If the Scriptures are timeless, then the Temple is timeless since it is *the* framework for the entire Bible.

The question we must ask is whether G-d's community, and in particular its leadership, is acting as a bride or a harlot. Have we joined ourselves in an unholy alliance with the world, especially in the financial arena? We could argue today's Babylon is "government." Has government become the foreign oppressor and the "beast?" Have we abdicated our responsibility to take care of the poor, the widow, the orphan, the fatherless, and the oppressed — handing it over to government? Have we remained silent in the face of over fifty-eight million abortions (in the US), courts sanctioning same sex-marriage, and the flourishing pornography and sex trafficking industry? Have we turned a blind eye to corruption and injustice? Are we, the faith community, to blame for the current state of things? If so, we have indeed placed ourselves under a heavy yoke and become slaves — no different from Israel in Egypt under Pharaoh. We have opened the door for "foreigners" to oppress G-d's people mainly because of our silence. We have been enticed by the harlot and eaten from the Tree of the Knowledge of Good and Evil.

The near obsession with the "end times" has paralyzed many from engaging with the culture and trying to make a difference. This preoccupation serves only to tickle ears and make some rich, famous, and popular in the Christian world. We don't know the future. But with the Wisdom he has freely given us, we can judge the future based on historical and biblical patterns.

Unfortunately, many have taken a more fatalistic approach — content to believe "the great tribulation" is upon us and there is nothing that can be done. Some behave as helpless automatons waiting for *Yeshua's* return. In doing so, we reject G-d's greatest gift to mankind: the ability to choose and to change.

The destruction of the Second Temple in the first century was the result of choices made by the leadership. It could have turned out differently had they chosen to repent and turn back to G-d.

The Temple reflected the spiritual condition of G-d's people. If we are indeed His "temple of the Holy Spirit," this has not changed. G-d will judge His own House using foreign oppressors. It is time for leaders to count the cost, to speak out against the evils of our day, and to take responsibility for their sheep. The prophets never held back their criticism of the shepherds who led the sheep astray, and G-d will certainly hold Christian leaders to account.

Christians now find themselves marginalized and exiled to the very fringes of society. Instead of retreating, it is time to step up, renew our relationship with G-d, and rebuild the House before it is destroyed like both the First and Second Temples. It is time to restore the unity of the seventh day and to see the Kingdom established on earth as it is in heaven. G-d's message is to look up for your redemption and to help those who are scattered come back to the sheepfold to be fed in green pastures (an idiom for the Temple). This task has been given to "His people" who are His Holy Temple: to be His hands extended throughout the earth.

> *May it be your will, HaShem our G-d and the G-d of our forefathers that the Holy Temple be rebuilt, speedily in our days. Grant us our share in your Torah and may we serve you there with reverence.*
>
> (*Y'hi Ratzon* PRAYER)

Choose Life or Death

> *How goodly are your tents, O Jacob, your dwelling places O Israel. As for me, through your abundant kindness I will enter your House; I will prostrate myself toward your Holy Sanctuary in awe of you. O HaShem, I love the House where*

you dwell and the place where your glory resides.

(Mah Tovu MORNING BLESSING)

In the world of the ANE, which includes the Bible, creation stories were connected to building a temple. "In the beginning" was not a chronology of events but rather temple building with G-d as designer and master craftsman. Together with Wisdom, G-d built His cosmic House. He established it through a covenant/oath based on seven declarations: the first seven words of the Bible. The covenant, akin to a marriage covenant, sealed the bonds between G-d and His creation. To build a house meant the uniting of masculine and feminine in order to produce offspring to continue the family line. "However, at the beginning of creation, G-d made them male and female" (Mark 10.6). Every "house" in the natural world was to follow the pattern set by the eternal world. "For ever since the creation of the universe his invisible qualities — both his eternal power and his divine nature — have been clearly seen, because they can be understood from what he has *made*" (Rom. 1.20).

The creation Temple's outer courtyard was the cosmos. The inner courtyard was the garden. The inner chamber was "in the midst" of the sanctuary where two trees stood: the Tree of Life and the Tree of the Knowledge of Good and Evil. The Tree of Life, pictured as the menorah, represented Wisdom, G-d's bride. The Torah was the personification of Wisdom and was the instruction manual for a healthy, functioning house. The Tree of Knowledge, on the other hand, represented Folly who was the harlot. The cosmos was created and maintained through sets of opposites so mankind could exercise free will to choose between Death and Life. The greatest gift G-d instilled in mankind was the ability to choose. In doing so, one's destiny may be determined. Both trees were considered *kedushah*, holy and set apart, because each had a specific function and role to play. Adam and Eve were not to eat fruit from the Tree of Knowledge. Eating its fruit caused their death: the opposite

SEVEN AND THE TEMPLE

of life. Death meant permanent separation and the inability to reproduce life. The great commission, on the other hand, was to "go and fill the cosmos with the Sons of G-d" and "to be fruitful and multiply and fill the earth" with life! This is temple building language.

The Bible tells the story of those who were called by G-d to rebuild His house and provide for His people. Noah built a boat to protect and preserve his family. The Patriarchs expanded their tents and in so doing built the House of Israel. Moses oversaw the building of the Tabernacle in the wilderness: the place where G-d would dwell in the midst of His people and become a hedge of protection for Israel from her enemies. Bezalel and Oholiav were the Tabernacle's master craftsmen. King David was given the blueprints for the First Temple through the Spirit of G-d. Solomon oversaw its construction and Hiram was its master craftsman. The Temple brought unity to the nation. When the exiles returned from Babylon, Ezra oversaw the construction of the Second Temple. This was a modest House in comparison to the glory of the First Temple. King Herod expanded that Temple to its greatest extent until it was destroyed by Rome in 70 CE. Out of the ashes of the physical Temple came a new spiritual house. It began with the resurrected body of *Yeshua* the Messiah. His House was based on the pattern of the previous "temples," but it was a living, breathing entity built through the Sons of G-d. This temple was also built on a foundation of precious jewels: the foundation of apostles.

In the original Tabernacle, the high priest sprinkled the blood of a bull and a goat on the *kapporet* and the *parokhet* in the Holy of Holies on the Day of Atonement. This ritual brought temporary restoration through the cleansing action of the blood, for it is "the blood" that sustains life! "For the life of the flesh is in the blood, and I have given it to you upon the altar to make atonement for your souls; for it is the blood that makes atonement for the soul" (Lev. 17.11 NKJV). The sprinkling of *Yeshua's* blood in the heavenly Holy of Holies permanently cleansed and restored the broken covenant. The New Covenant, that is, the restored Creation Covenant, was achieved through his blood. *Yeshua* prophesied, "Destroy this temple and in three days I will raise it up again" (Jn. 2.19). He was speaking of "his body" (21). He had been sent by his Father to rebuild the "fallen *sukkah*" and to re-establish the broken bonds of the original covenant through blood.

Paul spoke of the redeemed community using temple building language: a new creation, a tent, a field, G-d's building, a house for the Spirit, and living stones. This was likely based on his understanding that "in the beginning" was the framework for G-d's cosmic House and that this pattern was replicated in the cosmos, the human family, the Tabernacle, the First Temple, the Second Temple, and the Body of Messiah.

> Therefore if anyone is united with the Messiah, he is a new creation — the old has passed; look, what has come is fresh and new!
>
> (2 CO. 5.17)

> We know that when the tent which houses us here on earth is torn down, we have a permanent building from G-d, a building not made of human hands, to house us in heaven. For in this tent, our earthly body, we groan with desire to have around us the home from heaven that will be ours.
>
> (2 CO. 5.1-2)

> For we are G-d's co-workers; you are G-d's field, G-d's building…I laid a foundation, like a skilled master-builder; and another man is building on it. But let each one be careful how he builds. For no one can lay any foundation other than the one already laid, which is *Yeshua* the

Messiah. Some will use gold, silver or precious stones in building on this foundation; while others will use wood, grass or straw. But each one's work will be shown for what it is, the Day will disclose it because it will be revealed by fire — the fire will test the quality of each one's work (This is the *Brit Esh* — the Covenant of Fire).

(1 CO. 3. 9-13)

Don't you know you people are G-d's temple and that G-d's Spirit lives in you? So if anyone destroys G-d's temple, G-d will destroy him. For G-d's temple is holy, and you yourselves, are that temple.

(1 CO. 3.16)

As you come to him, the living stone, rejected by people but chosen by G-d and precious to him, you yourselves, as living stones, are being built into a spiritual house to be *Kohanim* set apart for G-d to offer spiritual sacrifices acceptable to him through *Yeshua* the Messiah.

(1 PETER 2.4,5)

Yeshua, the son of the master craftsman, was filled with the wisdom, knowledge, and understanding needed to rebuild G-d's House. He entered the world outside of time, rebuilt the cosmic Temple, and took his seat on the throne next to the Father to rule and reign in justice and righteousness and mercy. He is the resurrection and the life. "In him was life, and that life was the light of mankind" (Jn. 1.4).

There is a man coming whose name is *Tzemach* [sprout]. He will sprout up from his place and rebuild the Temple of *Adonai*. Yes he will rebuild the Temple of *Adonai*; and he will take up royal splendor, sitting and ruling from his throne.

The message of G-d's House is life and life everlasting. Therefore...CHOOSE LIFE! Build your house and reproduce fruit after your own kind for the sake of the Family of G-d! Choose Wisdom — it is the truth that will make you free!

I call heaven and earth as witnesses today against you, that I have set before you life and death, blessing and cursing; therefore choose life, that both you and your descendants may live, that you may love the Lord your G-d, that you may obey His voice, and that you may cling to Him, for He is your life and the length of your days; and that you may dwell in the land which the Lord swore to your fathers, to Abraham, Isaac, and Jacob, to give them.

(DEUT. 30.19-20 NKJV)

EPILOGUE

O our king and our G-d, cause your Name to be unified in your world; rebuild your city, lay the foundation of your house, perfect your sanctuary, gather in the scattered exiles, redeem your sheep and gladden your congregation....

Although our journey together in search of the purpose and function of the Temple has been thought-provoking and perhaps at times a bit overwhelming, the core message of this book, dear reader, is truly a simple one: It is about building a house and a family and bringing forth new life. This was made crystal clear in my last days of writing.

As I was finishing my work, my very dear friend Monica was battling one of the greatest scourges of our day: cancer. I am grateful to have had the chance to speak to her on the phone before she began to lose consciousness. I asked if she would share some thoughts with my readers about how her relationship with G-d and her Messiah had deepened through this difficult journey. Unfortunately, that never happened. There was an event at the hospital, though, which proved providential.

Monica's daughter asked her if she understood what was happening around her. "Can you hear the family talking and praying?" "Are you talking with G-d?" "What is going through your mind?" Monica answered that her mind would be completely quieted, and then she would hear a voice. The voice would ask her to make a choice between life and death! Monica explained that when she chose life everything went quiet again. She heard the same question asked several times: "Do you choose life or death?" At first she felt almost annoyed. Repeatedly she chose life, and the quiet returned. We all assumed, of course, that choosing "life" meant life here on earth, but the opposite now seems more likely. The life that she was choosing was eternal life in His heavenly House.

It was a Sunday afternoon when a petite, elderly woman entered the hospital room to clean. She never uttered a word. She just cleaned and then left. A moment later, however, she returned. In a barely audible voice, she said, "G-d is listening, and He is the Breath of LIFE." With that she departed again. Monica's daughter raced to the door and glanced up and down the hall in both directions — there was no one to be found. She hurried to the nurse's station to inquire about this "housekeeper" but was told that no one cleaned the rooms on Sundays. It seemed a messenger from outside of time, from the throne room of Heaven, brought the Word of the Lord: CHOOSE LIFE! He is life; He is the breath of life and the very air that we breathe! It is only He who can make this life bearable and prepare us for the next!

Monica was fiercely determined to live. She spent her last month in the hospital fighting for her life. Every day was a roller coaster between improvement and setbacks. After the staff removed her feeding tube, everyone prepared to let her go. By the next day, however, she had regained some of her strength and had become more alert. Her kidney function returned, and the puffiness left her face. She was clearly determined to celebrate her young son's seventh birthday that was only a few days away. Her final wish was to leave the hospital to be with her family at home. The Father honored that desire; she died peacefully — surrounded by those she loved the most.

Monica made her peace and entered that secret, intimate place with Him — under His wings in the shelter of His loving arms — the place of the Holy of Holies where angels sing and rest comes. She would be the first to tell you to nurture your closest relationships and to extend daily love, mercy, and compassion to those around you. I am only the vessel called by G-d to write about that secret place. Monica, on the other hand, is the one who has actually experienced it. And so I dedicate this work to her. You have entered His rest, my dear friend; I will see you in Glory!!

It is the Spirit who gives life; the flesh profits nothing. The words that I speak to you are spirit, and they are life.

JOHN 6.36

BIBLIOGRAPHY

Apocrypha and Pseudepigrapha of the Old Testament (2004), 2 vols, ed. R.H. Charles, Berkeley: Apocryphile Press.

Babylonian Talmud (1935-52), 35 vols, London: Soncino Press.

Barker, M. (1995) *On Earth as it is in Heaven: Temple Symbolism in the New Testament*, Edinburgh: T&T Clark.

_____ (2000) *The Revelation of Jesus Christ*, Edinburgh: T & T Clark.

_____ (2004) *Temple Theology*, London: SPCK.

_____ (2007) *Temple Themes in Christian Worship*, London: T & T Clark.

_____ (2008) *The Gate of Heaven: The History and Symbolism of the Temple in Jerusalem*, Sheffield, England: Phoenix Press.

_____ (2010) *Creation: A Biblical Vision for the Environment*, London: T & T Clark.

_____ (2011) *Temple Mysticism: An Introduction*, London: SPCK.

Beale, G.K. (2004) *The Temple and the Church's Mission: A Biblical Theology of the Dwelling Place of G-d*, Illinois: Inter Varsity Press.

Benner, J. A. (2005) *The Ancient Hebrew Lexicon of the Bible*, College Station, TX: Virtualbookworm.com publishing.

Bereishis (1986) 2 vols, Brooklyn: Mesorah.

Berlyn, P. (2005) *The Journey of Terah: To Ur-Kasdim or Urkesh*, Vol. 33, No. 2 Jewish Bible Quarterly.

Berman, J. (1995) *The Temple: Its Symbolism and Meaning Then and Now*, Eugene, OR: WIPF and Stock Publishers.

Brooke, G. J. (2005) *Dead Sea Scrolls and the New Testament*, Minneapolis: Fortress.

Briggs, R. A. (1999) *Jewish Temple Imagery in Book of Revelation*, NYC: Peter Lang.

Charlesworth, James H. (1985) *The Old Testament Pseudepigrapha*, 2 vols,

Garden City: Doubleday.

Clements, R. E. (1965) *G-d and Temple*, Oxford: B. Blackwell.

Clorfene, C. (2005) *The Messianic Temple: Understanding Ezekiel's Prophecy*, Jerusalem: Menorah Books.

Culi, Y. (1989) *The Torah Anthology: Me'am Lo'ez Leviticus-I*, trans. A. Kaplan, Brooklyn: Moznaim.

Danby, H. (reprinted 1989), *The* , trans. H. Danby. Oxford: Oxford University   Press.

Daube, D. (1998) *The New Testament and Rabbinic Judaism*, Peabody, MA: Hendrickson.

De Vaux, R. (1973) *Ancient Israel: Its Life and Institutions*, London: Darton, Longman & Todd.

Dever, William G. (2005) *Did G-d have a Wife?: Archaeology and Folk Religion in Ancient Israel*, Grand Rapids: William B. Eerdmans.

DeConick, April D. (2011) *Holy Misogyny: Why the Sex and Gender Conflicts in the Early Church Still Matter*, NY: Bloomsbury.

Dictionary of Deities and Demons in the Bible (1995), 2nd ed., Van Der Toorn, Becking, Van Der Horst. Grand Rapids: Wm. B. Eerdmans.

Day, John (1986) *Asherah in the Hebrew Bible and Northwest Semitic Literature*, Oxford: Oxford University Press.

Edersheim, A. (1994) *The Temple: Its Ministry and Services*, Peabody, MA: Hendrickson.

Falk, H. (2002) *Jesus the Pharisee*, Eugene, OR: WIPF and Stock Publishers.

Fisher, Loren (1963) *Temple Quarter*, Journal of Semitic Studies 8 (Spring)

Flusser, D. (2009) *Judaism of Second Temple Period*, 2 vols, Grand Rapids: William B. Eerdmans.

Fox, Michael V. (2000) *Anchor Yale Bible: Proverbs 1-9*, New Haven, CT: Yale University Press.

Good, Joseph (2015) Measure the Pattern Volume I: *A study of the Structures Surrounding the Inner Courtyard of the Temple*, Nederland, TX: Joseph Good

Ginsburgh, Y. (1991) *The Alef Beit: Jewish Thought Revealed through the Hebrew letters*, Northvale, NJ: Aronson.

Ginzberg, L. (1909-38) *Legends of the Jews*, 7 vols.

Heschel, A. J. (1975) *The Prophets*, 2 vols, NY: Harper.

Hurowitz, V. (1992) *I Have Built You an Exalted House: Temple Building in the Bible in Light of the Mesopotamian and Northwest Semitic Writings*, Sheffield, England: Academic Press.

_____ (1985) *The Priestly Account of Building the Tabernacle*, Journal of the American Oriental Society, 105.1.

Instone-Brewer, D. (2004) *Traditions of Rabbis from the Era of the New Testament: Prayer and Agriculture*, Grand Rapids: William B. Eerdmans.

Interlinear Chumash (2008) 5 vols, Artscroll Series, Brooklyn: Mesorah.

Keil and Delitzsch (2011) *Commentary on the Old Testament: Isaiah, Vol. 7*, trans. James Martin, Peabody, MA: Hendrickson.

Kline, M. (1999) *Images of the Spirit*, Eugene, OR: WIPF and Stock Publishers.

Kitov, E. (1997) *The Book of Our Heritage: The Jewish Year and its Days of Significance*, 3 vols, Jerusalem: Feldheim.

Levenson, J. D. (1985) *Sinai and Zion: An Entry into the Jewish Bible*, New York: Harper & Row.

Lundquist, John M. (2008) *The Temple of Jerusalem: Past, Present, and Future*, Westport, CT: Praeger.

Marcus R., and Thackeray, H. St. J. (1927) *Josephus*, 12 vols, Loeb Classical Library, Cambridge MA: Harvard University Press.

Meshel, Ze'ev (1979) *Did Yahweh have a Consort?* Vol. 5, No.2, Mar/Apr. BAR.

Midrash Tanchuma (1935) 2 vols, Jerusalem: Eshkol.

Milgrom, J. (2004) *Leviticus*, Minneapolis: Fortress.

Mishnah Seder Mo'ed Vol. 2 (1984), trans. P. Kehati, Israel: Maor Wallach Press

Mishneh Torah (English), trans. Eliyahu Touger, Chabad.org

Moore, G.F. (1997) *Judaism in the First Centuries of the Christian Era*, 2 vols, Peabody, MA: Hendrickson.

Morrow, Jeff (2009) *Creation as Temple-Building and Work as Liturgy in Genesis 1-3*, Journal of the Orthodox Center for the Advancement of Biblical Studies 2, no. 1.

Mowinckle, Sigmund (2004) *The Psalms in Israel's Worship*, Grand Rapids: William B. Eerdmans.

Munk, M. L. (1983) *The Wisdom in the Hebrew Alphabet: The Sacred Letters as a Guide to Jewish Deed and Thought*, Brooklyn: Mesorah.

Nickelsburg, George W.E. & Vanderkam, James C. (2004) *1 Enoch: A New Translation*, Minneapolis: Fortress.

Oliver, Isaac W. (2013) *Simon Peter Meets Simon the Tanner: The Ritual Insignificance of Tanning in Ancient Judaism*, Cambridge: Cambridge University Press.

Patai, R. (1947) *Man and Temple in Jewish Myth and Ritual*, NY: KTAV Publishing.

_____ (1979) *The Messiah Texts*, Detroit: Wayne State University Press.

_____(1990) *The Hebrew G-ddess*, 3rd edition, Detroit: Wayne State University Press.

Patai, R. & Graves, R. (1964) *Hebrew Myths*, NYC: Doubleday.

Patterson, David (2005) *Hebrew Language and Jewish Thought*, NY: Routledge.

Raanan, Y. *The incense Altar and the Menorah*, Chabad.org.

Rashi (1972) *Commentary on the Torah*, 5 vols, trans. M. Rosebaum and N.M. Silbermann, Jerusalem: Silberman.

Revelation (1975) trans. by J. Massyngberde Ford, New Haven, CT: Yale University Press.

Rittmeyer, L. (2006) *The Quest: Revealing the Temple Mount in Jerusalem*, Jerusalem: Carta.

Stern, D. (1992) *Jewish New Testament Commentary*, Clarksville, MD: Jewish New Testament Publications.

Schwartz, H. (1993) *Gabriel's Palace: Jewish Mystical Tales*. NY: Oxford University Press.

Temple in Antiquity (1984) ed. T. G. Madsen, Salt Lake City, UT: Bookcraft.

The Apocryphal New Testament (2004) trans. M.R. James, Berkeley, CA: Apocryphile Press.

The Aryeh Kaplan Anthology (1975), 2 vols, Brooklyn: Mesorah.

The Complete Artscroll Siddur (1985), Brooklyn: Mesorah.

The Old Testament Pseudipigrapha (1983-85), ed. J. H. Charlesworth, 2 vols, Garden City, NY: Doubleday.

The Works of Josephus (2000), trans. W. Whiston, Peabody, MA: Hendrickson.

The Works of Philo (1993), trans. C.D. Yonge, Peabody, MA: Hendrickson.

Tosefta (2002), 2 vols, trans. J. Neusner, Peabody, MA: Hendrickson.

Trumball, H. C. (1975) *The Blood Covenant*, Kirkwood, MO: Impact Books.

_____ (2000) *The Threshold Covenant*, Kirkwood, MO: Impact Books.

Van Leeuwen, Raymond C. (2007) *Cosmos, Temple, House: Building and Wisdom in Ancient Mesopotamia and Israel*, ed. Richard Clifford, *Wisdom Literature in Mesopotamia and Israel*, No. 36, Atlanta: Society of Biblical Literature.

Vayikra (1989), Brooklyn: Mesorah.

Vermes, Geza (1981) *Jesus the Jew*, Philadelphia: Fortress.

_____ (1997), *The Complete Dead Sea Scrolls in English*, London: Penguin.

Walton, J. H. (2006) *Ancient Near East Thought and the Old Testament*, Grand Rapids: Baker Books.

_____ (2009) *The Lost World of Genesis One: Ancient Cosmology and the Origins Debate*, Illinois: Inter Varsity Press.

Weinfeld, M. (1981) *Sabbath, Temple and the Enthronment of the Lord – The Problem of the Sitz im Leben of Genesis 1:1-2:3.*

Widengren, G. (1951) *The King and the Tree of Life in Ancient Near East Religion*, Uppsala: Lundequist.

Yechezkel (1977), Brooklyn: Mesorah.

GLOSSARY

Acharei Mot - After death, Torah portion: Leviticus 16
Acharit haYamim - end of days, the future
Adam - blood of G-d
Adamah - red, earth, ground
Adonai - Lord, substitute for YHVH
Aharon - Aaron
Ahzar - help
Ana Beko'ach - We beg you
ANE - ancient near east
Aravot - seventh heaven, willows, valley in the Negev
Argamon - purple
Aron - Ark
Asherah - tree, mother goddess
Ashrei - praiseworthy, honorable
Avram - Abram
Avraham - Abraham, father of many
Azarah - courtyard

Ba'al - master, Canaanite god
Bamot - high places
Bar - grain
Barah - to create
Barah Shtei - created two
Bat - daughter
Bat Kol - daughter of the voice
Batsheva - daughter of seven, Bathsheba
Bavel - Babylon, Chaldea
Beersheva - well of seven or oath, city in the Negev
Beit Avtinas - house of Avtinas, incense producers
Beit HaParvah - house of the tanning of the hides
Beit - house

Beit haMikdash - House of the sanctuary
Beit Rosh - house is head
Ben - son
Benai - children, plural of son
Beresheet - in the beginning, Genesis
Binah - understanding
Brit - covenant, to cut
Brit Chadasha - renewed covenant, new covenant, New
    Testament
Brit Esh - Covenant of Fire
Brit Milah - covenant of cutting, circumcision
BT - Babylonian Talmud

Chavah - Eve
Chachmah - wisdom
Chag haMatzah - Feast of Unleavened Bread
Charan - city in northern Mesopotamia
Cheruv - cherub
Cheruvim - two angelic figures atop the Ark of the Covenant
Chilazon - snail
Chokmah - wisdom
Chol HaMoed - intermediate days for the festivals of Passover
    and *Sukkot*
Cohen - priest
Cohanim - priests plural

Da'at - knowledge
Debir - Holy of Holies
Devar - speak
Devorah - bee, community

Eish - man
Eishah - woman
Eishet Chayil - Woman of Valor, Proverbs 31
Elisheva - my G-d is seven, Elizabeth

Elohim - name for G-d, plural of El

Eretz - earth, land

Etz Chaim - Tree of Life

Etz Shemen - oil tree

Erusin - second stage of marriage

Esh - fire

Even Shettiyah - foundation stone, stone of drinking

Ezrat Kohanim - Courtyard of Priests

Ezrat Nashim - Courtyard of the Women

Ezrat Israel - Courtyard of Israel

Gan Eden - garden in Eden

Genizah - burial place

Gihon - belly, gush, womb, spring in Jerusalem

Haftarah - passage from prophets read after the Torah

HaKodesh - the Holy Place

Hakhel - gathering

Har - mountain

HaShem - The Name used as a substitute for G-d's name in conversation

Hekal - sanctuary

Hoshanna rabbah - great salvation

Hoshen - breastplate of the high priest

Ya'acov - Jacob

Y'itzchak - Isaac

Kadosh - holy, set apart, separate

Kaf - palm, shovel for the incense

Kal - complete

Kallah - bride

Kapporet - cover

 - sanctified, dedicated, consecrated, set apart (can also be a harlot)

Kiddushin - betrothal stage of marriage
Ketoret - incense
Kodesh - holy
Kodesh haKodeshim - Holy of Holies
Kohanim - plural for priests
Kohen - priests
Kohen Gadol - High Priest
Kol - voice
K'por - frost

Lashon Harah - evil tongue
Levonah - frankincense
Levon - white
Livyathan - Leviathan
Luchot HaEven - Tablets of Stone

Ma'aleh Ashan - smoke rising herb
Ma'amad - standing ones
Ma'aseh Merkavah - works of the chariot
Malkat Sheva - Queen of Sheba
Malkut - kingdom
Malkut Shemayim - Kingdom of Heaven, Kingdom of G-d
Mashal - parable, proverb, dominion, rulership
Maschiach - messiah
Matzah - unleavened bread
Mayim - water
Mayim hayim - living water
Melech - king
Menorah - seven-branched lampstand
Midrash - interpretation
Mikvah - immersion bath
Minchah - afternoon prayer service, gift, grain offering
Miriam - Mary
Mikdash - Holiness
Mikvah - immersion bath

Mishkan - Tabernacle
Mislei - Proverbs
Mitzvot - commandments
Mizbeach - altar
Mizrak - vessel used to carry the blood
Moshe - Moses

Nach - strike

Ohel Moed - Tent of Meeting
Olam Haba - eternity, the World to Come
Olam Hazeh - This World, physical world
Or - light
Oren - pine tree

Palhedrin – a chamber in the Temple
Parokhet - curtain, veil
Pargod - a curtain from the Persian language
Pelusium - Egyptian term for white garments of fine linen
Pesach - Passover

Rach - to follow a prescribed path
Rachaf - to hover, move, flutter as a bird
Rachav - proud, Rahab
Racham - mercy
Rakiah - firmament, expanse
Rav Sha'ul - Rabbi Paul
Rosh - head
Rosh Chodesh - new moon, head of the month
Rosh HaShanah - New Year's, head of the year
Ruach - spirit
Ruach Elohim - Spirit of G-d
Ruach HaKodesh - Holy Spirit

Seraphim - burning

Shacharit - morning, morning prayer service
Shalach - send out
Shabbat - Sabbath, seventh, rest
Shavua - week
Shavuot - Feast of Weeks, Pentecost
Shekan - to dwell
Shekinah - divine or indwelling presence
Shem HaMeforash - ineffable name
Shema - hear, Hear O Israel - opening words of the prayer
    proclaiming the unity of G-d
Shemayim - heavens
Shemot - Exodus
Sheva - seven, oath
Sheish - linen, six
Shiloach - pool of sent
Shitin - shafts
Shlomo - Solomon
Sh'mittah - seventh year of release for the land
Shofar - ram's horn trumpet
Shtei haLechem - two breads
Siddur - Hebrew prayer book
Simcha Beit haShoevah - Rejoicing in the House of the
    Water Drawing
Sukkah - booth, temporary shelter
Sukkot - Feast of Tabernacles

Tahor - pure
Tamai - impure, contaminated
Tanakh - Old Testament
Targum - Aramaic paraphrase of the Hebrew Bible
Techelet - blue dye from Chilazon, a sea mollusk
Tehillim - Psalms
Tehom - the waters of the deep, the abyss
Terach - Abraham's father
Teruah - blast of the shofar

Teshuvah - repentance

Tevillah - immersion

Tikun Olam - restoring the universe

Tisha B'av - ninth day of the fifth month Av

Tishri - seventh month on Hebrew calendar, usually in Sept./Oct.

Tolat Sheni - crimson red dye from a worm

Toldot - generation, history, account, to bear children

Tov - good

Tov Ma'od - very good

Torah - instruction, law, first five books of the Bible

Tzaddik - righteous one

Tzitzit - fringes knotted in a special way and attached to a four cornered garment

Tziyon - Zion

Tzemach - sprout

Ulam - porch in the temple

Yam - sea

Yehoshua - Joshua

YHVH - unpronounceable name of G-d, tetragrammaton

Yireach - moon

Yom - day

Yom haKippurim - Day of Atonements

Yom Echad - One day or Day One

Yom Teruah - Day of the Blast of the Shofar

Yeshua - Jesus

Yocheved - Glory of Yah

Zekan - elder

Zerah - seed

Zevach - sacrifice

Z'kharyah - Zechariah

Zur - scattered or estranged

THE TEMPLE REVEALED
IN THE GARDEN

In *The Temple Revealed In The Garden*, Dinah Dye takes us on a journey to the Garden Sanctuary. Adam and Eve are serving as priests in G-d's Sacred Space. The reader will discover how Adam functioned as high priest as he "worked" and "guarded" the garden, how he dressed in the priestly robes, and how he ministered in the priestly office. The meaning behind familiar symbols such as the Tree of Life and the Tree of the Knowledge of Good and Evil will be explored in vivid detail. Other temple topics include the menorah, the threshing floor, the seed, the burnt offering, and the Foundation Stone. Discover answers to some of the Bible's most perplexing questions as we visit the Garden of Eden in the next exciting volume.

ABOUT THE AUTHOR

Dr. Dinah Dye was raised in Ottawa, Canada, in a conservative Jewish home. She attended Hebrew school, celebrated the festivals with her family, and enjoyed summers at an Orthodox Jewish summer camp. Dinah spent her teen years and early twenties deeply involved in the New Age movement. During those years, she came to the belief that truth would be based on three things: it would be easy to understand, it would be for everyone, and it would be based on love. She met that truth in 1979 in *Yeshua* (Jesus) the Messiah.

Dinah immediately recognized the importance of connecting the Gospels and the Epistles to their proper foundation in the Torah (first five books of the Bible). That understanding eventually led to the creation of her ministry Foundations in Torah. Dr. Dye holds a DMIN in Hebraic Studies in Christianity and has been uncovering Hebraic connections for over 35 years. Dinah's teachings can be found in both audio and video formats, and she speaks regularly at conferences and for local congregations throughout the United States and internationally.

Dinah's real passion is to help students of the Bible research and understand the Hebraic nature of the New Testament Scriptures. Much of Dr. Dye's latest research revolves around The Temple. She suggests the Temple is the framework for the entire Bible and holds an important key for bringing unity to a fractured community.

Foundations in Torah
www.FoundationsInTorah.com
dyedinah@gmail.com
drdianadye@gmail.com
PO Box 1098
Placitas, NM 87043